Interviewing in Community Oral History

COMMUNITY ORAL HISTORY TOOLKIT

Nancy MacKay • Mary Kay Quinlan • Barbara W. Sommer

This five-volume boxed set is the definitive guide to all aspects of successfully conducting community projects that conform to best practices in the field of oral history. What are the fundamental principles that make one oral history project fly and another falter? The existing oral history methodology literature has traditionally focused on conducting academic research. In contrast, the *Toolkit* is specifically geared toward helping people develop and implement oral history projects in schools, service agencies, historical societies, community centers, churches, and other community settings. The five concise volumes, authored by leaders in the oral history field, offer down-to-earth advice on every step of the project, provide numerous examples of successful projects, and include forms that you can adapt to your specific needs. Together, these volumes are your "consultant in a box," offering the tools you need to successfully launch and complete your community oral history project.

Volume 1: *Introduction to Community Oral History*, by Mary Kay Quinlan with Nancy MacKay and Barbara W. Sommer

Volume 2: *Planning a Community Oral History Project*, by Barbara W. Sommer with Nancy MacKay and Mary Kay Quinlan

Volume 3: *Managing a Community Oral History Project*, by Barbara W. Sommer with Nancy MacKay and Mary Kay Quinlan

Volume 4: *Interviewing in Community Oral History*, by Mary Kay Quinlan with Nancy MacKay and Barbara W. Sommer

Volume 5: *After the Interview in Community Oral History*, by Nancy MacKay with Mary Kay Quinlan and Barbara W. Sommer

For additional information on this series, visit www.LCoastPress.com.

Community Oral History Toolkit

NANCY MACKAY • MARY KAY QUINLAN • BARBARA W. SOMMER

VOLUME 4

Interviewing in Community Oral History

Mary Kay Quinlan

with Nancy MacKay

and Barbara W. Sommer

Left Coast
Press Inc.

Walnut Creek, California

LEFT COAST PRESS, INC.
1630 North Main Street, #400
Walnut Creek, CA 94596

Left Coast
Press Inc.   www.LCoastPress.com

Library of Congress Cataloging-in-Publication Data

MacKay, Nancy, 1945-
  Community oral history toolkit / Nancy MacKay, Mary Kay Quinlan, and Barbara W.
Sommer
    5 v. ; cm.
  Includes bibliographical references and index.
  Contents: v. 1. Introduction to community oral history / by Mary Kay Quinlan with
Nancy MacKay and Barbara W. Sommer -- v. 2. Planning a community oral history
project / by Barbara W. Sommer, with Nancy MacKay and Mary Kay Quinlan -- v.
3. Managing a community oral history project / by Barbara W. Sommer with Nancy
MacKay and Mary Kay Quinlan -- v. 4. Interviewing in community oral history / by
Mary Kay Quinlan with Nancy MacKay and Barbara W. Sommer -- v. 5. After the
interview in community oral history / by Nancy MacKay with Mary Kay Quinlan and
Barbara W. Sommer.
ISBN 978-1-59874-408-8 (complete set - pbk. : alk. paper) -- ISBN 978-1-61132-688-8
(complete set - consumer ebook) -- ISBN 978-1-61132-241-5 (volume 1 - pbk. : alk.
paper) -- ISBN 978-1-61132-689-5 (volume 1 - consumer ebook) -- ISBN 978-1-
61132-244-6 (volume 2 - pbk. : alk. paper) -- ISBN 978-1-61132-690-1 (volume 2
- consumer ebook) -- ISBN 978-1-61132-247-7 (volume 3 - pbk. : alk. paper) -- ISBN
978-1-61132-691-8 (volume 3 - consumer ebook) -- ISBN 978-1-61132-250-7 (volume
4 - pbk. : alk. paper) -- ISBN 978-1-61132-692-5 (volume 4 - consumer ebook) -- ISBN
978-1-61132-253-8 (volume 5 - pbk. : alk. paper) -- ISBN 978-1-61132-693-2 (volume
5 - consumer ebook)
  1. Oral history--Handbooks, manuals, etc. 2. Oral history--Methodology. 3.
Interviewing--Handbooks, manuals, etc. 4. Local history--Methodology. I. Quinlan,
Mary Kay. II. Sommer, Barbara W. III. Title.
  D16.14.M22 2012
  907.2--dc23
                        2012026513

Contents

Author's Preface

This volume of the *Community Oral History Toolkit* represents nearly 40 years of accumulated experience as a newspaper reporter, a college journalism teacher, an oral historian, oral history workshop presenter, and oral history college teacher, the latter in concert with my colleague and friend Barbara Sommer. Along the way, many people have taught me about the art of interviewing, including:

- Don Ferguson, my high school journalism teacher, who taught me the value of asking people questions and listening to their answers;

- politicians I've interviewed who have mastered the art of saying a lot, but never really answering a question;

- Martha Ross, who introduced me to oral history methodology in a graduate history course at the University of Maryland;

- Donald A. Ritchie, Anne Ritchie, and Sara Collins, my oral history mentors and friends; and

- hundreds of presenters at Oral History Association conferences over the past 20 years whose work reflects some of the best work being done in this evolving field.

And my work on the *Community Oral History Toolkit* with Barbara Sommer and Nancy MacKay has challenged me to analyze the oral history interviewing process in even greater detail. Few people are privileged to enjoy such a collaboration among friends.

But most of all, my interest in interviewing stems from my passion for history, the stories of how things used to be and why they matter. And for that, I owe a debt of gratitude to my late parents, Paul and Ilene Quinlan.

They raised me and my sisters in a household that valued stories, from family lore to current events. They connected us to those who came before us, and they taught us to connect to those who will come after. I only regret that I couldn't record all of their stories.

Mary Kay Quinlan

Series Introduction

Every community has them. The people who remember

- what happened when the church burned to the ground on Christmas Eve—how the congregation grieved, and then set aside its grief, got to work, and celebrated in a new sanctuary the next year;

- how strangers with pickup trucks took tornado victims to the nearest hospital when a record-breaking storm devastated the community;

- what it was like to bring a neighborhood together to fight the city's plans for a freeway; or

- how children, teachers, and community members felt the first day black and white youngsters shared the same classrooms in the aftermath of all the lawsuits attempting to block school integration.

Old newspaper clippings tell part of the story. So do public records that document the storm, the cost of neighborhood redevelopment, or the text of the court's decision. But what's often missing from the record is the *human* side of the issues, events, and ideas that we call history. And if you're reading the *Community Oral History Toolkit,* there's a good chance you already are thinking like an oral historian. You understand that it's important to add to the historical record first person information that can flesh out or reshape our understanding of past events.

Collectively, we three *Toolkit* authors have spent more than half a century working with community oral history projects, observing along the way how some succeed and others languish. You can readily find an excellent body of literature on oral history methodology, but it is designed for academic research and often does not translate well for unaffiliated community groups. So we've attempted in this five-volume *Toolkit* to identify some fundamental principles that lead to successful community oral history projects and to present practical tools and guidelines that we hope will be useful in a variety of community settings.

Defining Oral History

We define *community* broadly, using the definition found in the Oral History Association's pamphlet *Using Oral History in Community History Projects* (2010). The pamphlet defines community as any group of individuals bound together by a sense of shared identity. For the purposes of this *Toolkit*, we consider community oral history as that being undertaken by any group unaffiliated with an academic institution. Such groups could be neighborhood associations, historical societies, museums, libraries, professional associations, clubs, or any of the myriad ways people organize themselves to accomplish particular ends. Because we consider *community* in its broadest sense, we've included examples of community oral history projects that are diverse in size, topic of study, sponsoring organization, geographic location, and project goals. As you move through your own oral history project, and through the five *Toolkit* volumes, we encourage you to define your own community in the way that works best for you.

Community oral history projects differ in many ways from those originating in an academic setting. They usually

- lack institutional support for planning, managing, or funding;

- are organized around an exhibition, festival, performance, or publication;

- are driven by grant cycles and deadlines, sometimes with a specific goal determined by the funder;

- are carried out by volunteers or by a single paid staff member supervising volunteers;

- barter with local businesses or agencies for office space, technology expertise, and supplies;

- lack infrastructure, such as office space, storage, and computer equipment; and

- almost always have limited funds.

This *Toolkit* recognizes the special challenges community oral historians face and suggests ways to deal with them. It is predicated on the notion that a well-funded institutional setting is not a prerequisite to create solid oral history projects that will endure over time. What is required, however, is a fundamental understanding of oral history as a process that begins long before you ask the first interview question and ends long after you turn off the recorder.

For starters, here's how oral history is defined throughout these five volumes.

Oral history is primary source material collected in an interview setting with a witness to or a participant in an event or a way of life and is grounded in the context of time and place to give it meaning. It is recorded for the purpose of preserving the information and making it available to others. The term refers to both the process and the final product.

What You'll Find in the *Community Oral History Toolkit*

The *Community Oral History Toolkit* consists of five individual volumes. Each volume covers a particular aspect of doing oral history. Although each volume stands alone, the *Toolkit* is best seen as an integrated reference set, in much the same way that any particular aspect of doing oral history is dependent on decisions made at other stages of the process. The *Toolkit* is tightly organized, with subheadings, cross references within the text, and a comprehensive index for ready reference. You'll also find various visual elements, including hot spots (concise tips), definitions, sidebars (case studies and extended discussions), checklists, and figures that illustrate, elaborate, or draw attention to specific points. While all three of us have collaborated throughout the project, we divided the writing duties for the five volumes. Barbara Sommer is the lead author of Volumes 2 and 3; Mary Kay Quinlan is the lead author of Volumes 1 and 4; and Nancy MacKay is the lead author of Volume 5 and overall project coordinator, spearheading the research phase, marshaling the final details and keeping us all on task.

Volume 1. Introduction to Community Oral History. This volume sets the stage for your oral history project. It introduces the field to newcomers, with a discussion of the historical process, the evolution of oral history as an interdisciplinary research methodology, the nature of community and the nature of memory, and the legal and ethical underpinnings of oral history. And as such, Volume 1 importantly lays the theoretical groundwork for the practical application steps spelled out in detail in the subsequent volumes. It also introduces recording technology issues and options for oral history preservation, access, and use. Last, this volume elaborates on our Best Practices for Community Oral History Projects and presents a detailed overview of the remaining *Toolkit* volumes.

BEST PRACTICES
for Community Oral History Projects

1. **Familiarize yourself with the Oral History Association's guidelines.** First developed in 1968 and revised and updated regularly since then, these guidelines are the benchmark for the practice of ethical oral history and form the foundation on which solid oral history projects are built. Becoming familiar with them will help your project get off to a strong start.

2. **Focus on oral history as a process.** Keep in mind that, using standard historical research methods, you are setting out to explore a historical question through recorded interviews, giving it context and preserving it in the public record—in addition to whatever short-term goals your project may have such as using interview excerpts to create an exhibit or celebrate an anniversary.

3. **Cast a wide net to include community.** Make sure all appropriate community members are involved in your project and have an opportunity to make a contribution. Community members know and care the most about the project at hand, and the more closely they are involved in every aspect of it, the more successful it will be.

4. **Understand the ethical and legal ramifications of oral history.** Oral historians record deeply personal stories that become available in an archive for access both in the present and the future. So oral historians have ethical and legal responsibilities to abide by copyright laws and respect interviewees' wishes while also being true to the purposes of oral history.

Volume 2. Planning a Community Oral History Project. This volume walks you through all the planning steps needed to travel from an idea to a completed collection of oral history interviews. It will help you get started on firm ground, so you don't end up mired in quicksand halfway through your project or trapped in a maze of seemingly unsolvable problems.

Volume 3. Managing a Community Oral History Project. This volume takes the planning steps and puts them into action. It provides the practical details for turning your plans into reality and establishes the basis for guiding your project through the interviews and to a successful conclusion.

Volume 4. Interviewing in Community Oral History. The interview is the anchor of an oral history project. This volume guides the interviewer through all the steps from interview preparation to the follow-up. It includes tips on

5. **Make a plan.** At the outset, define your purpose, set goals, evaluate your progress, and establish record-keeping systems so details don't get out of control.

6. **Choose appropriate technology with an eye toward present and future needs.** Technology is necessary for recording interviews, preserving them in an archive, and providing access and using them for public displays. Make wise decisions about the technology you use.

7. **Train interviewers and other project participants to assure consistent quality.** Oral history interviews differ from some other interview-based research methods in the amount of background research and preparation required. Make sure interviewers and other personnel are thoroughly trained in oral history principles, interviewing techniques, recording technology, and ethics. The *Community Oral History Toolkit* covers all these topics.

8. **Conduct interviews that will stand the test of time.** This is the heart of the oral history process, but its success depends on laying solid groundwork.

9. **Process and archive all interview materials to preserve them for future use.** Oral history interviews and related materials should be preserved, cataloged, and made available for others to use in a suitable repository, such as a library, archive, or historical society.

10. **Take pride in your contribution to the historical record.** Share with the community what you've learned, and celebrate your success.

selecting interviewees, training interviewers, using recording equipment, and assessing ethical issues concerning the interviewer-interviewee relationship.

Volume 5. After the Interview in Community Oral History. Community projects often falter after the interviews are completed. This volume explains the importance of processing and archiving oral histories and takes readers through all the steps required for good archiving and for concluding an oral history project. It finishes with examples of creative ways community projects have used oral histories.

Finally, sample forms, checklists, and examples from the experiences of other community projects are provided that will help guide your project planning and a selected bibliography that will lead you to additional in-depth information on the various topics covered in the *Toolkit*.

We hope you will keep these volumes close at hand as you work step by step through your oral history project. Remember that the effort you put into doing the project right will pay off in unexpected ways far into the future. Many years from now you may well remember the exact words, tone of voice, or facial expression of an interviewee in answering questions only you thought to ask. And you may take satisfaction in knowing that your effort has preserved an important story—a piece of history that gives meaning to all our lives, both now and in the future.

Nancy MacKay, Mary Kay Quinlan, and Barbara W. Sommer

Toolkit Contents

CHAPTER 1

What, Exactly, is an Oral History Interview?

BEST PRACTICE NO. 1

Familiarize yourself with the Oral History Association's guidelines.

BEST PRACTICE NO. 2

Focus on oral history as a process.

Stop! Don't turn on your recorder.

The interview is the centerpiece of an oral history project, and this volume will help you learn effective interviewing techniques. But you're not ready to start recording until you've satisfactorily answered all of the following questions.

- Have you created a project team and chosen a project director to ride herd on the project?

- Have you decided on a focus for the project?

- Have you named the project?

- Have you identified people in the community who can support and advocate for the project?

- Have you decided on the project scope, including planned programs, publications, or other outcomes?

- Have you figured out the timeline for project completion?

- Have you estimated the number of interviews you'll complete?

- Have you written a mission statement?

- Have you determined record-keeping procedures?
- Have you figured out a budget?
- Have you determined what recording equipment you'll use?
- Have you trained project volunteers?

You'll find details about each of these steps in **Volume 2,** *Planning a Community Oral History Project* and **Volume 3,** *Managing a Community Oral History Project.* Here's why checking them off matters. If you launch your oral history project merely with the notion that a particular person or group of people in your community have great stories to tell or important experiences to recount, and you rush to begin recording them, then what? Would you be able to answer the following questions?

- How will you decide which people in the community to interview?
- What questions will you ask after the interviewee finishes reciting her rehearsed tale?
- What will you do with the interviews after you have them?
- Will you have the legal authority to use the copyrighted interviews?
- Did you even know the interviewee had a copyright to his words?
- Will anyone else be able to hear your interviews?
- Will you transcribe them so others can read them?
- If so, who will do that? The interviewer? Someone else?

Once you've figured out answers to these and other questions by following the steps outlined in the **Planning (2) and Management (3) volumes** of the *Community Oral History Toolkit,* you'll be on your way to laying the groundwork for solid oral history interviews. And if you follow the steps in **Volume 5,** *After the Interview in Community Oral History,* your interviews will stand the test of time.

So let's get started. Oral history projects can document the history of a community or neighborhood, including the stuff of everyday life. They can collect memories of specific external events, whether natural or manmade disasters or notable landmark occasions in a community's life. Or they can focus on documenting the history of community institutions like churches, cultural centers, civic organizations, advocacy groups, or businesses. This volume of the *Community Oral History Toolkit* is based on the premise that you already have completed a thorough plan for your oral history project, whatever its focus, and that you have a management structure of some kind—ideally a handful of dedicated leaders with clear duties assigned and processes in place. Now, based on that plan, we'll take a look at what you need to do before an oral history interview, during the interview, and immediately after the interview, regardless of any plans your group may have to create special public programming based on the content of the interviews that you conduct.

Here is an outline of the activities in each phase of the interviewing process that will be discussed in detail in the rest of this volume.

WHAT PROJECT TEAMS NEED TO DO

Before the interview

✓ Develop background research materials for interviewers.

✓ Create a timeline, as appropriate, for the project's focus.

✓ Identify potential interviewees and contact them about the project.

✓ Recruit and train interviewers.

✓ Match interviewers with interviewees.

WHAT INTERVIEWERS NEED TO DO

Before the interview

✓ Become familiar with the project and its goals.

✓ Get training so you can use the equipment and learn interviewing techniques.

✓ Do general background research about the project's topic and specific research about your interviewee.

✓ Prepare an outline of topics to pursue in the interview.

✓ Use appropriate recordkeeping forms developed for your project to document information about your interviewee and the interview process and to secure the interviewee's consent.

✓ Schedule the interview.

✓ Arrive on time and bring everything you need.

✓ Arrange the interview setting to achieve the best possible audio or video quality.

During the interview

✓ Make sure the interviewee is comfortable.

✓ Check your equipment to be sure it's working properly.

✓ Record a standard introduction.

✓ Use the topic outline to guide questions.

✓ Ask follow-up questions for details and context.

✓ Use appropriate oral history interviewing techniques.

After the interview

✓ Sign the interview Legal Release Agreement.

✓ Photograph the interviewee.

✓ Thank the interviewee.

✓ Write a summary of the interview.

✓ Complete all remaining interview-related tasks as determined by the project team.

So please resist the temptation to turn on your recorder just yet. You have much to accomplish before you're ready to delve into the interview itself. And this volume will help you with those challenges.

Understanding Oral History Interviews

Shoe salesmen, police officers, supermarket clerks, teachers, doctors, scientists, moms, and oral historians all have at least one thing in common: they all ask questions. But the way they go about asking those questions—and listening to the answers—may be quite different. Some, like the shoe salesman, police officer, supermarket clerk, and doctor, often want to know something very specific: What size do you wear? What color do you like? Did you find everything you need today? Do you know how fast you were driving? Where does it hurt? For the scientist, questions may evolve from a hypothesis she is trying to test. For a teacher, questions may range from the specific—Did you do your homework?—to more general—What were the most important ideas in this chapter? And moms, of course, ask all kinds of questions—long, short, specific, wide-ranging, even unwelcome. Most people, in fact, are probably accustomed to asking and answering all kinds of questions throughout a typical day and taking various kinds of actions based on the answers to the questions they encounter. But to the oral historian, questions take on a uniquely important status, because they shape the oral history interview, giving it structure and focus. In an important sense, the interviewer's questions are what make each oral history interview unique.

The term "oral history" has acquired a popular, generic meaning referring to almost any circumstance—recorded or not—in which people talk about the past. Such discourse can be interesting, entertaining, tear-jerking, therapeutic, sentimental, and lots of fun. It can even reveal important, previously unshared, information about past times and places. But this *Toolkit* uses a more specific definition of oral history, aimed at assuring that collecting oral information about the past is accomplished in a systematic way that will yield depth and nuance to our understanding of past times and places and that it will remain available to the community for generations to come.

 An oral history interview is grounded in context of time and place.

In this *Toolkit,* an oral history interview is defined as one that is:

- structured,
- recorded,
- intended to elicit firsthand information,
- based on research that provides context, and
- made available to others.

As the definition suggests, an oral history interview is the co-creation of an interviewer and an interviewee, selected because he or she can recount firsthand information that will be kept permanently and be made publicly available. In other words, the oral history recording and its transcript become raw materials providing information and insights through which historians can understand and interpret the past. Oral histories serve as primary sources in the same way government documents, maps, diaries, letters, speeches, newspapers, photographs, minutes of meetings, and all manner of artifacts shed light on past times and places. But what sets oral history apart from these other kinds of documentary evidence is the ability of oral history interviewers to ask probing follow-up questions that enable an interviewee to go beyond creating lists of facts and figures.

Probing questions enable interviewees to go beyond lists of facts and figures.

Instead, a well planned and executed oral history interview will open windows onto the thoughts and feelings of the players in past times and places and generate reflections not only on *what* happened, but *why* it happened and *how* it affected people's lives.

An oral history interview is not:

■ an equal sharing of experiences and opinions,

■ a group discussion,

■ an accusatory inquisition,

■ a passive recital of reminiscences about the olden days,

■ a debate,

■ an argument,

■ a deposition,

■ a lecture, or

■ a reading from a diary or other documents about the past.

In its generic sense, the term "oral history" is often associated with popular recording projects like StoryCorps, the traveling road show in which people pay a fee to record a 40-minute interview with a loved one, sometimes using questions StoryCorps suggests. The term also is used to refer to other situations in which people self-select to record their memories at state fairs, museums, public commemorative events or similar occasions at which a recording booth or table is set up to gather brief stories or recollections volunteered by participants.

None of this is oral history, as this *Toolkit* uses the term. Here's why. These exercises, though they often collect interesting information, are seldom based on rigorous planning or research about the subject at hand or the particular individual being interviewed, and they almost always lack historical context. For example,

■ Just who is this person who came forward to tell his story?

■ Was the person in a position to have firsthand information about the events she describes?

■ What were the circumstances under which the recording took place?

Perhaps the interviewee's son just died in Afghanistan. Maybe she was just diagnosed with inoperable cancer. Did the interviewee just discover that the grandfather he despised has left him a big inheritance? Did she just sell to a big developer the family farm she so lovingly recalls? Is the interviewee at the church centennial celebration the congregation's biggest benefactor?

An oral history interview that will stand the test of time would answer all those questions, providing, in other words, some historical context that would add meaning to the interviewees' words.

More Than Turning On a Recorder

"There's a mindset that's palpable with those who have not been involved in a large oral history project that suggests oral history is simply taking a recorder into the field and spending a few hours with someone. On the contrary, helping interviewers understand 'their' role (not simply gathering information, but developing rapport and the consequences of that rapport) was a true challenge."

El Toro Marine Corps Air Station Oral History Project[1]

One final point about understanding what exactly an oral history interview is—and isn't. Television documentaries and other similar multimedia programming increasingly make use of rich sources of recorded interviews about the past, either created specifically for the program, snipped from speeches or broadcast interviews, or mined from oral history collections. The interviews in such documentaries and similar programs often appear to be tightly scripted and slickly produced. But what ends up on your screen usually represents only a tiny fraction of an entire interview, oral history or otherwise. Interview segments are selected by a producer specifically to highlight the key elements of the storyline being conveyed. So when you conduct an oral history interview, don't worry about false starts or repetition or some backtracking to fill in holes or long pauses or answers that seem to go far afield. Your interview is creating raw material, the primary document that you and others may then use to create subsequent public programming. It will not, and should not, look like a slick final product in itself.

 Your interview is raw source material and won't be a slick final product.

Remember, when you embark on an oral history interview, that raw material you're creating is the stuff of memory, a complex and controversial field of scientific research, as outlined in **Volume 1,** *Introduction to Community Oral History.*

Oral historians experience firsthand the variability of human memory. The following characteristics of memory play a key role in oral history interviews.

- People who have been in the same place at the same time will have different memories of an event because they experience it within their own frame of reference and accumulated life experience. In short, your particular memories are a function of who you are—your age, sex, ethnic background, family make-up, educational experiences, and countless other variables. Exploring those differences—and similarities—in perspective is what enables an oral historian to go beyond the superficial facts and draw a more nuanced, deeper understanding of the time and place in question.

- Memory is sometimes said to be "collective." That is, an individual's memories can be influenced by public discourse about events in a community. The challenge for oral historians is to go beyond those expressions of collective memory—the public stories that *everyone* supposedly believes—to unearth deeper layers of understanding about the past.

- Particular sounds, odors, and visual cues can trigger memories for some people, so it's sometimes useful for an interviewer to use maps, photographs, or other prompts to engage an interviewee or to ask what a particular place smelled or sounded like.

- The ability to recall a particular time, place, or event is not the same as an ability to articulate this memory. Furthermore, oral historians may encounter interviewees who are able to articulate their memories but who are unwilling to do so, perhaps because of perceived embarrassment, emotional pain, or a conviction that bygones should be bygones.

- Older interviewees in particular may find it easier to recall and describe long-ago events than recent ones.

- For other people, long-ago events may be foggy in memory, displaced by more recent—or more personally important—experiences.

- The well prepared oral history interviewer who can help an interviewee focus intently on the time and place in question often can elicit memories the interviewer forgot he had. Rare is the experienced oral historian who hasn't heard an interviewee say, "Wow! I haven't thought about that for ages. I had no idea I could remember all that."

■ People reinterpret their experiences—and their memories—in the light of new experiences or events. An occurrence that seemed life-altering when it happened may have proved to be much less significant in hindsight. Exploring such reinterpretations can be a rich line of questioning for oral historians.

These and other characteristics of memory are important for oral historians to consider as they embark on a community oral history project, for it sometimes happens that interviewees will recount something that couldn't literally be true. And occasionally, an interviewee will be adamant that his account is, indeed, correct. Don't be dismayed or dismiss the interviewee as a liar. Rather, such departures from your preconceived sense of the community's collective memory, or even from the literal accuracy of names and dates and places, illustrate the value of oral history in expanding our ability to understand the past. An oral history interview, ideally, will not be a mere recitation of historical facts. Rather it will be facts *plus* the meaning an interviewee assigns to those facts—how she understands them as part of the community's life and of her own.

Now that we've established what an oral history interview is, the next chapter will examine some fundamental ethical principles that underlie oral history.

CHAPTER 2

Understanding the Ethics
of Oral History Interviews

BEST PRACTICE NO. 4
Understand the ethical and legal ramifications of oral history.

When you conduct oral history interviews, you are asking people to give you something no one else can: pieces of their memories, their firsthand accounts of their experiences, their perceptions, their ideas. The ethical framework of oral history interviewing is based on respect for these interviewees and their stories.

 The ethical framework of oral history interviews is based on respect for the interviewee.

Alongside the ethical framework are legal issues that emerge because of an oral history interview's status as a copyrightable document under copyright law in the United States and many other countries, in much the same way that an autobiography, a musical composition, a stage play, or other kind of intellectual property can be copyrighted.

Volume 2, *Planning a Community Oral History Project*, includes a thorough discussion of the ethical as well as legal considerations oral historians face. You can also find important and useful information in *A Guide to Oral History and the Law*, by John A. Neuenschwander (see Further Reading). This chapter will highlight ethical and legal considerations related to the oral history interview itself, and should not be construed as offering legal advice for oral history projects as a whole.

An oral history interviewer will encounter ethical considerations at virtually every stage of preparing for the interview, conducting it, and following up afterwards. The following three sections address these considerations.

The Ethical Dimensions of Preparation

People who agree to share part of themselves in an oral history interview deserve to be treated with respect. For the interviewer, that means a commitment to learn:

- about the project and its purpose,
- how to operate the recording equipment, and
- techniques for conducting an oral history interview.

Volunteer interviewers who go into an interview without a clear understanding of what the oral history project is trying to accomplish and only the vaguest idea of how to operate the recording equipment are showing disrespect for the interviewees who have agreed to participate. Moreover, although interviewers often believe that they know how to ask questions and can conduct an interview, if the result is merely a series of unfocused, monosyllabic answers to historically irrelevant questions, they end up wasting the interviewee's time and their own. So project teams have an obligation to make appropriate training opportunities available to interviewers, and interviewers have an obligation to attend these sessions and learn all they can, no matter how much pre-existing knowledge or experience they think they have. And they have an obligation to use that knowledge to fully inform prospective interviewees about how the oral history process works.

Interviewers also have an ethical obligation to conduct thorough, objective research that will enable them to develop appropriate questions. They need to be willing to set aside preconceived notions about the subject at hand and pursue lines of questioning that may be controversial or may contradict prevailing views of the situation.

Oral history projects sometimes face a challenge of partnering with another community organization or a funding source that has a specific agenda or is seeking only positive public relations outcomes from its participation. Project teams and interviewers need to guard against slanting interviews or declaring certain aspects of a subject off limits for discussion as a concession to such partners or funders.

Sometimes community oral history projects start with a particular social or political agenda in mind, with the intent to use information collected from interviewees to further those ends. Such projects, by definition, do not set out to explore all aspects of often controversial issues, nor do they cast a wide net in incorporating community members with disparate views, which this *Community Oral History Toolkit* advocates. If public advocacy is the overt purpose of your project, the ethical choice would be to articulate that from the beginning and make sure everyone knows you purposely set out to tell only one side of a story.

Don't Let Interest Groups Shape Oral History Outcomes

"Remain scrupulously unbiased in conducting your interviews so that people will feel free to be honest with you about their experiences and ideas. Be wary of (and resist) ways in which various interest groups may try to shape the process or outcomes of your oral history collecting."

Susan Becker, Maria Rogers Oral History Program, Rocky Flats Oral History Project[2]

Interviewees' Memories Often Vary

A Greenwich, CT, project to document the history of Tod's Point illustrates the value of oral history projects designed to involve many interviewees rather than limiting them to people with the same views. The Greenwich interviewees offered varied—and delightful—descriptions of J. Kennedy Tod, who owned the site for many years.

- Arne Larsen recalled, "Mr. Tod was born in Scotland. He was average tall, and he had a goatee."
- Walter Lucas recalled, "I knew Mr. Tod. He was a little thin man, but he was funny. He used to say, 'Misturr Lucas, how's the burrds?' Oh, did he have a Scottish accent! He loved animals, and he wouldn't let anybody shoot a duck if he could help it. He was a nice man."
- Clyde Ford recalled, "Mr. Tod was a short little man. Scotch. His face just like a beet. Got the money, though."

Tod's Point, Greenwich, CT: An Oral History (The Greenwich Library, 2000)[3]

Because oral history interviews open windows onto past times and places, interviewers have an obligation to document the context from which the interviewee is speaking. What was the interviewee's connection to the time and place in question? What are the current circumstances in which the interview is taking place? Answers to such questions provide critical contextual information that will enable future users of the interviews to draw their own understandings of that earlier time and place.

Add Context to Help Future Users of Interviews

Worcester Women's Oral History Project interviewer Hanna Solska added important contextual information about her interview with the elderly May O. White in Oxford, MA. The beginning of the interview transcript contains the following note:

"I arrived to the home of Mrs. White with my friend Dr. Alicja Rudnicka, who is Mrs. White's physician and who arranged this interview. We agreed that she will leave after introductions; however on the insistence of Mrs. White, she stayed during the interview. Present during the interview also was Mrs. White's caregiver, Carol, who helps May from time to time to hear and understand my questions. After few minutes of set-up, we started the interview."

The interviewer included the following additional note at the end of the transcript:

"May called me on 8/22/2011 to add to her story this important information about Clara Barton. Clara Barton was May's grandmother's aunt with whom she lived since an early age. Therefore, she inherited many memorabilia of Clara Barton. May's family donated the house which became the Clara Barton Birthplace Museum, and its furnishings and personal items. May was involved with the museum from its inception serving on its board, volunteering and driving other volunteers to serve as docents and guides."

May O. White interview transcript, Worcester Women's History Project[4]

The Ethical Dimensions of Interviewing

A fundamental sense of respect for the interviewee and her story should underlie every oral history interview. That respect extends to basic behaviors—like arriving on time and appropriately attired for the interview and exhibiting a friendly demeanor—as well as to more complex interactions—like waiting quietly and respectfully when the interviewee sheds tears over memories that evoke strong emotions. Chapter 5 discusses interviewing techniques in detail, but from the beginning of the process, interviewers need to keep clearly in mind that oral history interviews can be intellectually and emotionally intense situations that require them to understand their role in the process. Specifically, an oral history interviewer is not a therapist, advice-giver, or debate opponent. Rather, the interviewer is the interviewee's partner in crafting an opportunity for the interviewee to relate and explore her own story, guided by informed questions from the interviewer, about historically interesting or important events, times, and places.

Interviews can evoke strong emotions. An interviewee sometimes will say after an interview that he really appreciated the chance to get something off his chest that has been bothering him for years. And, depending on the nature of the subject, it's not unusual for an interviewee to become emotional and shed some tears. Such intense reactions may illustrate the interview's therapeutic value for those particular interviewees. But keep in mind that such mental health outcomes are not the purpose of the interview.

The biggest challenge for some interviewers is to refrain from engaging in arguments with interviewees, particularly when an interviewee's assessment of the topic at hand is widely at variance with the interviewer's. Rather than argue, the ethical interviewer will ask follow-up questions, ask for clarifications, and pose questions as a devil's advocate to explore all aspects of the controversy. That's what adds the human dimension to what otherwise might be dry, factual accounts of the situation in question and is, in fact, the value of using oral history to document community history.

 Don't engage in arguments with interviewees.

While oral history interviewers never should shy away from asking about controversies, they also should not encourage interviewees to engage in idle gossip. And they should be alert to the possibility that an interviewee's words might be construed as slander against another person. If that does occur, interviewers have an obligation to notify the project director, who then may decide to restrict access to such an interview. Occasionally, interviewees themselves will request that access to some of the things they say about other people or situations be restricted, and project teams should honor such requests. See the *Toolkit* **Volumes 2, 3** and **5** for a complete discussion of these issues and how to handle them.

It's worth noting that oral history interviews aren't legally protected from disclosure. Unlike a husband who cannot be forced to testify in court against his wife or a pastor who cannot be forced to testify against a parishioner, oral historians enjoy no such legal protection. So while an archivist or librarian may honor an oral history donor's request not to make restricted interviews available to researchers, there generally is no such protection in the event such an interview is subpoenaed.

 Oral history interviews aren't legally protected from disclosure.

The Ethical Dimensions of Post-Interview Tasks

An interviewer's ethical obligations also extend to the administrative tasks necessary to complete the interview process. Attention to detail in handling paperwork, summarizing interview content, and transcribing are all part of respecting an interviewee's story by making sure it will become available for others to use and not just languish in a shoebox under someone's bed.

Community oral history projects sometimes go off the rails, when once-enthusiastic volunteers wander away and fail to follow through on the post-interview tasks that take a project to completion. Project directors then become frustrated in trying to track down missing pieces from volunteers who no longer are part of the project. If you're a volunteer interviewer, don't be one of those people. And if you're a project director—volunteer or otherwise—try to stay positive and keep everyone interested. It's no different from dealing with volunteers in Boy Scouts, church groups, parent-teacher associations, youth soccer, or any of the myriad organizations and activities that rely on the good will and enthusiasm of a volunteer workforce. Let people know what they're getting into, set performance standards, and become a cheerleader.

Finally, after the interview and the paperwork are over, consider one further ethical responsibility. In most cases, the oral history interviews you conduct will not become part of the public record until they are accessioned into a library, archive, museum, or other repository or posted on a website where they may be accessible to others for research or for public exhibit. (See the discussions in **Volume 2**, *Planning a Community Oral History Project*; **Volume 3**, *Managing a Community Oral History Project*; and **Volume 5**, *After the Interview in Community Oral History* for more information on this process.) Until then, it is inappropriate to chat with your family, friends, and co-workers about the great community history tidbits you learned from your oral history interviewees. Contributing fodder to neighborhood gossip is certainly not one of the purposes of doing oral history, and interviewers who engage in such activity could do irreparable damage to the project's efforts.

Legal Considerations

In addition to being conscious of the overarching ethical concerns, oral history interviewers need to understand the legal dimension of an oral history interview. **Volume 2,** *Planning a Community Oral History Project* and **Volume 3,** *Managing an Oral History Project* discuss this in detail, but interviewers as well as project teams need to understand that the participants in an oral history interview—both interviewer and interviewee—have created a copyrighted document as soon as the recorder is turned off.

Ballentine's Law Dictionary defines **copyright** as "the exclusive privilege...of an author or proprietor to print or otherwise multiply, publish, and vend copies of his literary, artistic, or intellectual productions, and to license their production and sale by others...."[6]

Copyright is governed by federal law, and you can find a detailed discussion of how copyright relates to oral history in Neuenschwander's *A Guide to Oral History and the Law*. But the bottom line is that both interviewer and interviewee essentially own their own manner of expression, in the same way that a person who writes her autobiography and publishes it in book form owns those words. Most oral history projects set out to collect information for archival purposes or to create public programming of some sort, but project sponsors cannot use oral history interviews for either of these purposes without the express permission of the interviewee and interviewer. At a practical level, that means projects generally ask oral history participants to sign Legal Release Agreements, sometimes called donor forms, giving their copyright interest in the interviews to the project. Otherwise, project sponsors or the repositories keeping the oral histories would have to go back to the oral history participants each time someone wanted to read a transcript, listen to an interview, or develop an exhibit using material from the interviews. That's why it's important for interviewers to have interviewees sign a Legal Release Agreement after each interview session—and sign it themselves—even if more interviews are planned with a particular individual. Figure 2.1, on page 36, provides an example of completed Legal Release Agreement.

Interviewers themselves may not be involved in developing the Legal Release Agreement for the project. It will help them explain the forms and the concept of copyright assignment, however, if the forms are written in plain, straightforward language, not complicated, hard-to-understand legalese. The historical society of one federal circuit court once began collecting oral history interviews with lawyers, staff members, and others who had long been associated with the court. But the effort was stymied because project volunteers, many of whom were themselves lawyers, had trouble agreeing on just what the multi-page, single-spaced form for the release agreement should include—an example of unnecessary overkill. What's important for the agreement is that the language clearly states the interviewee's and interviewer's intent to convey their copyright interests to the oral history project or the repository where the project materials will reside.

 A Legal Release Agreement should be concise and straight-forward.

Special Challenges and Restricted Interviews

When developing these release agreements, oral history projects sometimes encounter challenges in allowing for interview content to be restricted and in explaining the purpose and limitations of such forms. In such cases, working with the repository where your interviews will reside can help resolve these issues.

One community oral history project encountered resistance from interviewees who either wouldn't sign a form transferring copyright or refused to participate in an interview if they had to transfer copyright. When the repository hired a new collections manager, she discovered the archives did not hold copyright to the interviews, so she mailed new forms to all the interviewees and interviewers who were still living and to the families of the deceased to gain rights to the collection. About ninety-five percent of the forms were signed and returned. The manager suggested that perhaps the willingness to sign release agreements now, but not a decade earlier, reflects greater community trust in the repository, which it lacked at the outset of the project. Perhaps also a better explanation of the process by the interviewers in the first place might have secured the copyright transfers from the beginning.

Oral history projects often include in the Legal Release Agreement a provision authorizing the interviewee to use the interview for her own purposes, even though she has conveyed her copyright to the project. This amounts to the project sponsors granting a license to the interviewee to use the copyrighted material, which is permitted under copyright law.

Legal Release Agreements can include provisions to restrict access to the interview or to portions of it until a particular date or to set other restrictions on use of the material. See Figure 2.2 on page 37 for an example and see **Volume 5, *After the Interview in Community Oral History*** for a discussion of handling restricted interviews.

Legal Release Agreements today generally are worded to make sure the interviewee knows Internet publication is a possible future use of the interview materials, even if the project has no current plans to use the Internet. But provision always should be made to allow interviewees to explicitly prohibit Internet publication if they so choose, and such requests should be honored.

Finally, these agreements may include a sentence notifying the interviewee that, while every effort will be made to comply with any restrictions the interviewee has requested, the repository may not be able to enforce the restrictions in the event the interview is subpoenaed. If the Legal Release Agreement itself does not include such a statement, interviewers should make sure interviewees understand that constraint.

Figure 2.1 is a simple, standard release agreement that conveys copyright to the sponsoring organization and authorizes the interviewee to use the material for his own purposes during his lifetime; Figure 2.2 is a similar agreement but also provides for adding restrictions. Note that in both samples the interviewer signs the same form as the interviewee, although the interviewer could sign a separate form similar to the one designed for interviewees. Forms for these two Legal Release Agreements can be found in **Volume 1, *Introduction to Community Oral History*** and online at www.LCoastPress.com (go to the *Community Oral History Toolkit* page).

Community oral history projects often look at Legal Release Agreements for other projects or they review sample forms like the ones the *Toolkit* provides or the numerous forms in Neuenschwander's book to develop appropriate release forms for their projects. The signed agreement is an important legal document that will accompany the interview throughout its life as a component of the completed oral history. So it's a good idea to be sure the form you use is tailored for your project's specific needs. Don't just copy another project's form without considering whether it's appropriate for your project. Oral history project teams can often find a pro bono legal adviser to review Legal Release Agreement forms and thus be sure they are accomplishing what the project intends to accomplish. Above all interviewers need to have a solid understanding of what the form means and why interviewees are being asked to sign it, and they also need to be able to explain it clearly to their interviewees.

SAMPLE—LEGAL RELEASE AGREEMENT

The mission of the _Jazz Atlanta Oral History Project_
(oral history project) is to document the history of _jazz in Atlanta in the context of Southern U.S. musical traditions between 1975 and 2010._
The major part of this effort is the collection of oral history interviews with knowledgeable individuals.

Thank you for participating in our project. Please read and sign this gift agreement so your interview will be available for future use. Before doing so, you should read it carefully and ask any questions you may have regarding terms and conditions.

AGREEMENT

I, _Joseph A. Browne_ , interviewee, donate and convey my oral history interview dated _(insert date)_ to the _Atlanta Public Library_ _(oral history project/repository name)._ In making this gift I understand that I am conveying all right, title, and interest in copyright to the oral history project/repository. I also grant the oral history project/repository the right to use my name and likeness in promotional materials for outreach and educational materials. In return, the oral history project/repository grants me a non-exclusive license to use my interview through my lifetime.

I further understand that I will have the opportunity to review and approve my interview before it is placed in the repository and made available to the public. Once I have approved it, the oral history project/repository will make my interview available for research without restriction. Future uses may include quotation in printed materials or audio/video excerpts in any media, and availability on the Internet.

INTERVIEWEE	INTERVIEWER
Name (print) _Joseph A. Browne_	Name _(print)_ _Lane Smith_
Signature _(sign form)_	Signature _(sign form)_
Date _(insert date)_	Date _(insert date)_

Figure 2.1. Sample—Legal Release Agreement

SAMPLE—LEGAL RELEASE AGREEMENT (RESTRICTIONS)

The mission of the <u>Jazz Atlanta Oral History Project</u>
(oral history project) is to document the history of <u>jazz in Atlanta in the context of Southern U.S. musical traditions between 1975 and 2010.</u>
The major part of this effort is the collection of oral history interviews with knowledgeable individuals.

Thank you for participating in our project. Please read and sign this gift agreement so your interview will be available for future use. Before doing so, you should read it carefully and ask any questions you may have regarding terms and conditions.

AGREEMENT

I, <u>Wesley A .Z. Jones</u>, interviewee, donate and convey my oral history interview dated <u>*(insert date)*</u> to the <u>Atlanta Public Library</u> *(oral history project/repository name)*. In making this gift I understand that I am conveying all right, title, and interest in copyright to the oral history project/repository. I also grant the oral history project/repository the right to use my name and likeness in promotional materials for outreach and educational materials. In return, the oral history project/repository grants me a non-exclusive license to use my interview through my lifetime.

I understand that I will have the opportunity to review and approve my interview before it is placed in the repository. My gift and the associated rights are subject to the following restrictions:

_____   May not be made available on the Internet

__X__   Public access may not be available until (date):

   <u>*(insert restriction end date)*</u>

_____   Other *(specify)* _____

INTERVIEWEE	INTERVIEWER
Name (print) <u>Wesley A. Z. Jones</u>	Name (print) <u>Charles Wilson</u>
Signature <u>*(sign form)*</u>	Signature <u>*(sign form)*</u>
Date <u>*(insert date)*</u>	Date <u>*(insert date)*</u>

Figure 2.2. Sample—Legal Release Agreement (Restrictions)

CHAPTER 3

Before the Interview: What Project Teams Need to Do

BEST PRACTICE NO. 7

Train interviewers and other project participants
to assure consistent quality.

Successful oral history projects usually reflect a well-oiled team effort. And long before you get to the point of actually turning on a recorder and asking the first question, members of the project team need to anticipate and address the needs of interviewers. The better prepared your interviewers are, the better will be the quality of the resulting interviews. This chapter assumes your project planners have already completed the sequence of steps outlined in **Volume 2:** *Planning a Community Oral History Project,* which lay the groundwork for the interviewing phase of a project.

WHAT PROJECT PLANNERS SHOULD ALREADY HAVE ACCOMPLISHED

✓ Created a project team and chosen a project director to manage the project

✓ Decided on a focus for the project

✓ Named the project

✓ Identified people in the community who can support and advocate for the project

✓ Decided on the project scope, including planned programs, publications, or other outcomes

✓ Figured out the timeline for project completion

✓ Estimated the number of interviews you'll complete

✓ Written a mission statement

✓ Determined recordkeeping procedures and developed appropriate forms, including the Legal Release Agreement

✓ Figured out a budget

✓ Determined what recording equipment you'll use

✓ Identified a repository for the oral history collection and determined how to handle memorabilia and other archival materials that emerge

Now it's time to move the project into the interview phase by completing a number of pre-interview tasks. This chapter will discuss each of the following tasks and show how thorough work at this stage will greatly improve the quality of your oral history interviews.

■ Develop background research materials for your interviewers

■ Create a timeline, as appropriate, for the project's focus

■ Identify potential interviewees and contact them about the project

■ Recruit and train interviewers

■ Match interviewers with interviewees

Develop Background Research Materials For Your Interviewers

Once project teams have determined the scope of the project, it's important to develop a bibliography of materials about the subject you intend to document. The team can circulate a reading list or even create a small lending library or reading room with a shelf or file drawers of background material that everyone associated with the project is expected to review. This serves several purposes. First, everyone in the project needs to be familiar with what is already on the record about your subject. The purpose of oral history, after all, is to document new information. Second, reviewing the public record about your subject is critical to determining what isn't known. What are the holes your oral history project can fill? You won't know what's missing unless you're familiar what's already available. Last, reviewing the information already available may help you identify potential interviewees.

Depending on the nature of your community and your project, your background materials may include books, magazine articles, newspaper clippings, scrapbooks, minutes of meetings, government documents, websites, personal files, letters, photos, and whatever other kinds of documentary evidence you can collect that relate to the subject you're pursuing. Some projects will be able to amass a lot of information; others won't. The important thing about this step is to get enough information to put your project into context but not so much that you get bogged down in minutiae. For example, if your project is about a local area that was the site of a German prisoner-of-war camp during World War II, you certainly don't need to read every book that has ever been written about World War II, or even about prisoner-of-war camps. But you should try to find background information like: how many such camps there were, when they were started, when they closed, how many local people they employed, what the buildings at the camp were like, and so forth. In other words, you need enough information about German POW camps in general that you'll be able to determine how your local camp was the same as or different from other such camps. That's what is meant by putting your project into a larger context.

Here's another example. Let's say your project is focused on documenting the history of a community group that formed many years ago to fight the destruction of an ethnic neighborhood for a freeway project. You certainly might be able to find books written about local opposition to building freeways in urban areas, and you might be able to find a great deal that has been written about urban ethnic neighborhoods in general. Some of that might be useful context for your project. But your research materials would probably rely heavily on scrapbooks of newspaper clippings, government records about the project, and the like. In this particular example, maps would be important to study, and project participants would want to familiarize themselves with the neighborhood, the proposed route, and its effect on the neighborhood. You'd want to concentrate on understanding what is already on the record about the community as well as what is on the record about the proposed freeway construction. In any case, be sure that those involved with the project have a chance to familiarize themselves with what's already known about your particular subject of inquiry.

 Don't get sucked into the black hole of Internet research.

A word of caution: Online research can quickly devour endless hours. You could spend the rest of your life Googling your subject and related research terms. Don't do that. The Internet is a wonderful tool to find information quickly, and it should greatly streamline the process of creating a bibliography for your project volunteers. But it likely will prove useless in trying to find local information about your specific topic. Instead, the most effective way of collecting background information is probably the old-fashioned method of just asking around. Local people with knowledge of your subject may be able to steer you to a wonderful cache of scrapbooks someone kept all these years. Or they may know which local government agency has the public records pertaining to your subject. Local newspapers and local historical societies sometimes write community histories that could contain useful background information. Libraries and county historical societies often keep subject files, clipping files, and photo files that can be treasure troves of information. And don't forget to ask the local newspaper about clipping and photo files that can help you learn more about the subject at hand.

Remember that the purpose of all this research is to provide the interviewer with sufficient background to understand what the interviewee is talking about. The interviewee no doubt will mention many people, places, and events related to the subject of the interview, and an interviewer who is familiar with those details, at least in general, will be able to ask appropriate follow-up questions, and also will know when a subject has been exhausted and it's time to move to other questions. Well-prepared interviewers also will be able to help an interviewee who can't recall a specific date or name, for example. Such preparation gives interviewers confidence that they know enough about the subject to ask intelligent questions that will get at new information the interviewee can offer. Interviewers should not, however, use their background knowledge to show off how smart they are by asking long, convoluted questions based on the details of their research. If the interviewer comes across as knowing everything there is to know about the subject at hand, the interviewee then may wonder what the point of the oral history interview is.

At some point in the search for background information, the project team will need to determine when enough is enough. The main thing to keep in mind is this: You never want interviewers to be in a position of going in cold to an interview. This always results in a disaster.

Create a Timeline

Project teams should have created a timeline for completing the overall project. But this timeline refers to a list of dates associated with key events related to the focus of your project.

Sample Project Timeline

Excerpt of a timeline from *The People Who Made It Work: A Centennial History of the Cushman Motor Works*[5]

1940   The company received a government contract to produce bomb nose fuses.

1943   Responding to the need for war materials, the company employed 750 people, more than twice as many as at any other time in its history. The company was given the Army-Navy "E" award for excellence in production and contribution to the war effort.

1944   Production of the Airborne model of motor scooter began as part of the WWII effort. Over 15,000 models of this scooter were produced; they were used by all branches of the armed services during the war.

1945   War production ended. In addition to the Airborne, the company produced 8,500,000 bomb nose fuses. At the height of the war effort, the plant employed 1,200 women working around the clock to produce the fuses.

1946   The "B" Building was built. The plant had a workforce of 400 people working two shifts a day.

Your timeline might be more or less detailed than the preceding example. It may have specific dates, not just years, when various events occurred, and it might include specific names of individuals involved in various activities or places where certain events occurred. But don't make the mistake of thinking that names, dates, and places are all that matter. Rather, the timeline is a tool project teams and interviewers can use to help figure out what the oral history interviews can illuminate. It becomes a building block for the interviews, and it can be an important reference for interviewers when an interviewee stumbles in trying to remember a specific time or event.

Occasionally, the oral history interviews themselves help fill in blanks in the timeline. In the Cushman oral history project, for example, it took a combination of documentary evidence, including aerial photographs of the plant and interviewees' recollections, to pin down the year that Cushman closed its foundry, which had once been considered one of the finest such shops west of Chicago.

Identify Potential Interviewees

Two important ground rules should guide your search for potential interviewees.

■ They should be individuals with firsthand knowledge of the time, place, or events you're trying to document.

■ They should have the ability to articulate their recollections.

Fulfilling these requirements sometimes can be trickier than it sounds. Some people are quite talkative and even are known as entertaining storytellers in the community. But do they have firsthand knowledge of the subject in question or is their information mainly secondhand? Other people might have been key players in the subject you're investigating, but age, infirmity, an inarticulate speaking style, or just plain inability to remember may prevent them from being effective as interviewees. So even if you are convinced that, for example, the founding president of the neighborhood association would be the perfect source, it may be that the vice president or secretary or some other founding member is actually better able to recount the stories about the early days.

Prominent People May Not Be Ideal Interviewees

Some community oral history projects face the awkward situation of needing to include as interviewees prominent people who may not meet the two criteria of having firsthand knowledge and having an ability to articulate it. Don't worry about it. Do the interviews, if it will prevent feathers from being ruffled. In the long run, it probably will benefit the project more to have those folks involved rather than to risk people feeling slighted, even if the interviews turn out to be virtually content free.

Project planners probably started a list of potential interviewees almost as soon as the idea for the project got off the ground. Indeed, many projects emerge from an awareness that so-and-so has great recollections of how things used to be and the realization that when he's gone, his storehouse of knowledge will be gone too. But you'll want to go beyond the names of people whom project team members already know firsthand. That's where the research phase—pulling together reference materials about the subject—comes in. As you read newspaper clippings, letters to the editor, minutes of city council meetings, or even an organization's newsletters and membership lists, for example, many names will emerge of people who were involved in the subject you're investigating, and you'll start to get a picture of the various players who might be able to shed additional light on the topic. Remember that the focus of oral history is to go beyond what's already on the record, so as you conduct the research, keep asking yourself, What's missing here? What questions haven't been answered? What should we be trying to find out? and Who would be in a position to fill in the blanks? Make notes to yourself as you go along, and think about what you still need to know. Sometimes, it will be specific names and dates, as in trying to determine when the Cushman foundry closed. But equally important is trying to find out why and how things happened as they did. Often, those are the most important historical questions, and answers only can be found through oral history interviews. Exploring why things happened as they did or how certain decisions were made or what being in a particular situation was really like can add depth and nuance to otherwise unadorned facts about the subject at hand.

 Oral history interviews go beyond facts to get at *why* **and** *how.*

Oral history project teams sometimes are tempted to advertise for potential interviewees. This is seldom a good idea. It may create a large pool of names, but people who respond to an ad are likely to believe you've made a commitment to interview them, even if it turns out they have little to contribute. Most projects have finite resources in terms of money and volunteer time, and it's inadvisable to spend those resources trying to winnow wheat from chaff. In the same vein, you may have a social media enthusiast among your project team who is keen to create a Facebook page or Twitter account for your oral history project. These outreach tools may be useful after you have something to talk about and something to show for your efforts, but at the outset, they are more likely to be an unnecessary distraction at best and, at worst, lead to losing control of the project in the face of unsolicited contributions.

Likewise, you should avoid the approach of simply taking your recorder to a location where people gather—a community center, farmer's market, or Sunday concert at the local band shell—in the hope that you'll find appropriate people to interview. Journalists use this approach to do unscientific, man-on-the-street polls, which often result in interesting news and feature stories. But oral historians who attempt such a scattershot strategy are doing a disservice to the concept of oral history and may well find they have expended considerable energy for limited results.

Note that the *Toolkit's* approach to researching potential interviewees and selecting them is dictated by the specific information they can contribute to the historical record for your project and thus is quite different from interviewing projects in which people self-select to be interviewed. Recording booths like StoryCorps or tables at commemorative events, museums, and the like, where people are invited to record their recollections of the subject, can yield interesting information. But unlike the oral history interviews advocated here, in which a thoroughly prepared interviewer asks questions of people who are in a position to know the answers firsthand, those kinds of informal recording sessions seldom provide enough context to contribute much to the historical record, entertaining as they sometimes may be.

It's OK to Be Selective in Choosing Interviewees

As you select interviewees, keep in mind that, just because someone has always been considered the go-to source for information about your topic, that doesn't mean you must interview that person. Perhaps he has already been interviewed extensively, or maybe she has written many books and articles outlining her views. What would an interview add? The Women in Journalism Oral History Project decided not to interview prominent Washington reporter Helen Thomas precisely for those reasons. Planners involved in that project determined that their resources would be better spent conducting interviews with other path-breaking women journalists whose careers were less well documented than Thomas's.

Once you've cast a wide net and developed a pool of potential interviewees, it's time to set some priorities and start contacting people to request interviews. Your list of potential interviewees likely will continue to grow as the research continues and interviews get underway. Some of your interviewees may alert you to other people whose names haven't surfaced but who would be useful sources. Add them to the list. You may not be able to interview everyone, but it never hurts to maintain a list of potential interviewees in case your project takes on a life of its own and that allows you to continue with additional resources. But if resources—both financial and human—are limited, you'll need to determine which potential interviewees are most important to seek out first. Actuarial considerations usually are critical, with priority given to those who are oldest or most infirm. But age and health are not the only considerations. Perhaps one potential interviewee goes to Florida for six months over the winter. You might want to schedule that interview before she leaves. Or perhaps another person is an accountant who has little spare time in the weeks leading up to April 15—Tax Day in the United States. It might be best to wait till he has a more flexible schedule and can devote time and attention to an oral history interview. Likewise, you might give priority to an interview with a key player who can shed more light on the subject and provide important additional background research for the rest of the interviews. The point here is to consider as many variables as is reasonable when setting your interview priorities.

Oral history project teams sometimes are tempted to schedule social events or other gatherings with the intent of conducting group interviews, with an eye toward getting the most out of limited interview time. While this could be a useful way to introduce the project to a group of potential interviewees, and it almost certainly would be a great way to celebrate the end of a project with all the people who were interviewed, it seldom is a useful way to conduct meaningful interviews. In any group of people, even if only a few, one or two of them almost always dominate the conversation, despite an interviewer's best efforts to solicit answers from everyone and keep the session on track. Also, if someone in the group has opinions or recollections that differ from the prevailing views being expressed, it's likely to be difficult for that person to challenge the others. Moreover, unless the session is recorded on video, it is extraordinarily difficult to transcribe interviews with multiple voices. So, while there might be a place for discussion groups as part of a community history project, they are unlikely to result in collecting meaningful oral history interviews.

Be Realistic About Interviewing Goals

Community oral history projects often begin with great enthusiasm and ambitious goals to interview dozens of players who can contribute to the storehouse of knowledge about your topic. That's terrific. But it's also important to be realistic about matching your resources—human and financial—to the task at hand. It's usually better to set an initial goal of completing a handful of solid oral history interviews that are fully transcribed and deposited in a repository than to set your sights on dozens of interviews that might take years to accomplish. Successful completion of just four or five solid interviews could spark further interest in your project and draw additional financial resources and volunteers who would be able to make ten or twelve more interviews a reality.

In most cases, the best way to initiate contact with potential interviewees is by letter rather than a phone call. As Martha Ross, an early leader in the Oral History Association, was fond of telling students: Almost no one is standing by their telephone waiting for a call to invite them to be interviewed for an oral history project. Nearly always a phone call interrupts something the person is doing, which may not be the ideal approach for springing a new idea. A letter, on the other hand, gives you a chance to explain succinctly what your oral history project is all about and why you'd like the person to be involved. The letter should not require the recipient to take any particular action. Instead, say that a volunteer interviewer will be calling within the week to answer any questions and make arrangements for an interview.

Then, make certain that your interviewers are reliable and do, indeed, call the potential interviewee to answer any questions about the project, explain the Legal Release Agreement, and, in some cases, get appropriate background biographical information. You may also choose to follow the telephone call with an additional letter from the interviewer, once a time and place for the interview have been set, just to confirm the details.

 Letters to potential interviewees should not list interview questions.

Letters to potential interviewees should not enumerate specific questions the interviewer plans to ask. Rather, a list of general topics you expect to cover in the interview is in order and may help get the interviewee started in thinking about the subject at hand. When presented with a specific list of questions in advance, some interviewees have been known to write out their answers and insist on reading them onto the recording. This is not an oral history interview.

In some situations, project teams might consider using email as a way to make initial contact with people in the interview pool. This might work if you had a reliable way to make sure you had correct email addresses. But emails tend to pile up unread or otherwise get lost in the shuffle, and they convey a lesser sense of importance than an actual letter on paper in an envelope. A polite business letter on letterhead stationery will represent your project as something important and worth the potential interviewee's attention.

In all cases, just use common sense about the best way to introduce your project to your potential interviewees. If they are illiterate or not conversant in the same language you are, sending a letter obviously isn't the best approach. Perhaps you'll want to seek the support of organizations or individuals who have access to or are part of the community of potential interviewees and enlist their assistance in introducing you to individuals you'd like to interview and in explaining the process to them. In all cases, be organized and professional, and you'll go a long way toward enlisting the support and cooperation of potential interviewees.

Sample Invitation Letter to Potential Interviewee

Jazz Atlanta Oral History Project
P.O. Box 123
Atlanta, GA 30310

Joseph A. Browne, Director
Jazz Atlanta Festival
246 Peach Street
Atlanta, GA 30310

Dear Mr. Browne:

The Jazz Atlanta Oral History Project has embarked on an effort to document the history of the Jazz Atlanta Festival, and because of your involvement with the festival, we hope you will agree to participate in an oral history interview.

We would like to talk with you about:
• your personal background
• your musical background
• your memories of how you first became involved with the jazz festival
• highlights of how your participation evolved
• any challenges you have faced in connection with the festival
• your reflections and assessment of your experiences with the Jazz Atlanta Festival.

The Atlanta Public Library has agreed to accept all the oral history interviews conducted for this project, and we will ask your permission to give your interview to the Library, too. We'll also give a copy of the interview to you and your family.

Lane Smith, one of our volunteer interviewers, will call you within the week to talk with you about our project, answer any questions you might have, and arrange a time for an interview.

Thank you for considering our request.

Sincerely,

Andrea Schmidt, Director
Jazz Atlanta Oral History Project

Recruit and Train Interviewers

Just as not everyone is a good candidate as an interviewee, neither is every willing volunteer a good candidate as an interviewer. Effective interviewers, whether they are members of the community or outsiders, are people who are willing and able to:

- learn about the oral history process and participate in interviewer training,

- conduct necessary background research to craft an effective interview,

- master the use of the recording equipment,

- engage with sincere interest in and curiosity about the interviewees' stories,

- set aside whatever preconceptions they might have about the subject at hand and remain objective,

- follow through reliably on all recordkeeping and other tasks associated with the interviewing process, and

- be circumspect about what they hear in an oral history interview and refrain from gossiping about interviewees and what they say.

But the single most important characteristic of effective interviewers is a willingness to listen. This skill is less common than you might think. Community oral history projects sometimes encounter a situation in which many volunteers step forward to participate as interviewers because they have a personal interest or stake in the project's focus. This, of course, is an important motivation and is better than having no volunteers. But it can pose a few challenges, particularly if the project has been designed to attract a wide range of people and document viewpoints and experiences that may differ from the commonly held version of events on which the project focuses.

Interviewers who themselves are players often find it difficult to listen carefully to an interviewee's point of view, because they are so eager to express their own views, which may or may not be the same as those of the person being interviewed. Such personal involvement on the part of an interviewer also can lead to an interview in which the two parties chat like old friends, exchanging short-hand information and comments without explanation or follow-up. The resulting recording is bound to leave others scratching their heads, if they aren't privy to the insider point of view reflected in the discussion. Or it could lead to an interview that's more like an argument between people with widely opposing views. And finally, some people just plain can't stop talking. They simply love to chat about times gone by. And when they do stop inevitably to take a breath, you know they're just thinking of the next thing they're going to say and are not listening to anyone else. Willing volunteer or not, such people are not good candidates as interviewers.

Sometimes people are eager to volunteer as interviewers for a community oral history project because they say they just love to hear stories about the past. But information elicited in oral history interviews often can be quite routine, lacking the drama and plotline that can develop around oft-told family stories handed down through generations. Interviewers who expect to hear a contemporary version of Laura Ingalls Wilder's *Little House* tales are sure to be disappointed after their first interview and may fall away from the corps of volunteers.

So what should project teams do? Consider several options. If the would-be interviewer is genuinely someone with firsthand information about the subject, she should be interviewed. In fact, having interviewers-in-training interview each other is a good way for them to practice. Importantly, it also allows project teams to say to them, "You've already been interviewed, and we've already got your information on the record. So when you go out to interview others, there's no need to add your own views during the interview. You've already shared them."

This is where an interviewer training session is critical. It will give project teams a chance to observe volunteers' skills and will give potential interviewers a firsthand look at the kind of skills they need to interview effectively. It will also allow volunteers a chance to hear examples of successful oral history interviews, so they can understand that interviews rarely are recitations of names and dates or homespun reminiscences that are the stuff of Thanksgiving dinner-table stories. People will often self-select out at this point, realizing they talk too much or don't listen carefully enough to spot areas for follow-up questions, or they had a mistaken notion of what oral history was all about. But that doesn't mean you should turn them away. Many project teams find other tasks for volunteers for whom interviewing isn't the best fit. Perhaps they can gather background information, perform secretarial functions, help with interview scheduling, or even learn how to transcribe interviews, although this, too, is a task that can be trickier than it seems. Community oral history projects don't like to turn away volunteers, but it sometimes requires creativity to get every volunteer in the right slot.

Training project interviewers is critical to the success of an oral history project. The length and intensity of interviewer training will depend on a number of factors, but at the very least, a three- or four-hour session is required to cover the basics. A daylong workshop will be even more effective, because it will provide more time for hands-on experience. In all cases, would-be interviewers should be required to attend. Plus, they should be expected to put in however much additional time they need to become thoroughly familiar with the recording equipment and commit to the necessary pre-interview preparation that will be outlined in the next chapter. Volunteers who say they want to be involved but who are unwilling to commit the time required should not be interviewers.

Some oral history project teams have found it useful to present a training workshop, have each person conduct at least one interview, either with an assigned interviewee for the project or with a fellow interviewer-in-training, and then send the recording to the oral history trainer for a critique. Interviewers then attend a refresher workshop where the trainer can reinforce effective interviewing techniques and answer further questions that inevitably come up after the field work has begun.

Interviewer training workshop agenda

Here's a suggested workshop agenda for training community oral history interviewers. Many project directors schedule a full day for this workshop, so they can discuss each item thoroughly and still have lots of time for interviewers to practice using the recording equipment.

1. *Introductions.* Give all participants a chance to introduce themselves and describe any previous experiences they might have had with oral history or other forms of historical research, for example, genealogy.
2. *Introduction to oral history.* Provide an overview of oral history process, define terms, and discuss legal and ethical considerations and the distinctions between oral history and other kinds of question-asking pursuits. Show examples. See **Volume 1** for details.
3. *Introduction to the project.* Review the project focus and mission statement, other players involved as advisers or in other roles, and the nature of the planning accomplished to date. This agenda item should include discussion of the ultimate disposition of project materials and might include a representative from museum, library, or other repository that will take the interviews and other materials the project may generate. And if oral histories are expected to be used for public presentations in the short term, that should also be discussed.
4. *Equipment.* See that trainees have hands-on experience learning to operate the recording equipment. Try pairing them, so each partner can practice being the interviewer and interviewee. Interviewers are seldom expected to provide their own equipment, so arrangements should be made for them to borrow project equipment for practice before they actually conduct an interview.

5. *Recordkeeping.* Review all of the recordkeeping tasks interviewers must complete, including Legal Release Agreement, Legal Release Agreement (Restrictions), Interviewee Biographical Profile, Photograph and Memorabilia Receipt, Interview Summary and any other such materials the project plans to use. See **Volumes 1, 2, and 3** for recordkeeping information.

6. *Planning the interview.* If the task of gathering background information is not yet completed, ask trainees to help brainstorm the development of themes to be pursued in the interviews. If project teams have already done that, focus on structuring interviews, which is discussed in detail later in this chapter.

7. *Interviewing techniques.* Present interviewing best practices, as described in Chapter 5. Build in time for sample interviews so trainees have hands-on experience. Also, demonstrate a model interview, as well as illustrating an interview gone bad because of ineffective questioning techniques.

8. *Post-interview tasks.* Review importance of signing the Legal Release Agreement, completing the Interview Summary form and any other paperwork tasks interviewers in the project are expected to complete. Chapter 6 and **Volumes 2, 3, and 5** discuss recordkeeping in detail.

9. *Letter of Agreement for Interviewer.* Explain that most oral history projects require each interviewer to sign a document acknowledging their understanding of the project goal and acceptance of the responsibilities that accompany interviewing. See Figure 3.1 on the following page for an example Letter of Agreement for Interviewer. This is the ideal time to ask each interviewer to sign one of these forms.

Interviewers should leave a training workshop knowing:

- the nature and purpose of oral history in general and this project in particular,
- how to get access to the recording equipment so they can practice using it,
- what kinds of paperwork, including the Legal Release Agreement, they are expected to manage,
- where to find reference materials so they can get necessary background information,
- how to structure an interview,
- what an oral history interview sounds like,
- techniques for effectively conducting an interview, and
- whom to ask for help if they encounter a snag.

LETTER OF AGREEMENT FOR INTERVIEWER

I, _Lane Smith_____, an interviewer for the
_Jazz Atlanta_____Oral History Project, understand and
agree to the following.

- I understand the goals and purposes of this project and understand I represent the oral history project when I am conducting an interview.

- I will participate in an oral history interviewer training workshop.

- I understand the legal and ethical considerations regarding the interviews and will communicate them to and carry them out with each person I interview.

- I am willing to do the necessary preparation, including background research, for each interview I conduct.

- I will treat each interviewee with respect, and I understand each interview will be conducted in a spirit of openness that will allow each interviewee to answer all questions as fully and freely as he or she wishes.

- I am aware of the need for confidentiality of interview content until such time as the interviews are released for public use per the repository's guidelines, and I will not exploit the interviewee's story.

- I understand my responsibilities regarding any archival materials or artifacts related to the interview that the interviewee may want to include in the interview process.

- I agree to turn all interview materials over to the repository in a timely manner and to help facilitate all necessary processing and cataloging steps.

INTERVIEWER	ORAL HISTORY PROJECT
Name (print) _Lane Smith_____	Name (print) _Andrea Schmidt,_____ _Project Director_____
Signature _(sign form)_____	Signature _(sign form)_____
Date _(insert date)_____	Date _(insert date)_____

Figure 3.1. Sample—Letter of Agreement for Interviewer

Match Interviewers with Interviewees

Pairing individuals in your pool of interviewers with your pool of interviewees can seem like a daunting task, but it need not be if you stay focused on the following two things:

- your project's overarching goals and how they might best be accomplished, and

- the fact that an oral history interview is a unique, subjective encounter between two people whose individual world views affect everything they do.

Matching interviewers and interviewees is not an exact science; there's no one right way to do it. But that doesn't mean the wide variability of human traits shouldn't be taken into account as well as the position of the interviewer and interviewee in relation to the topic at hand. An interviewer who is an outsider, for example, someone not involved with or only tangentially involved with the community your project aims to document, might have to work harder to establish credibility with her interviewees. An interviewer who is an insider, on the other hand, someone who is part of the community being studied, may have to work harder at setting aside personal views or preconceived notions and being open to alternative explanations his interviewees may offer.

Ideally, all of your interviewers will be people who can pleasantly engage with someone who may be a stranger. Likewise, all of your interviewees presumably are willing to be interviewed, or they would not have agreed to participate in the first place. But project teams should strive to avoid pairings in which they suspect personalities would clash to the detriment of the interview quality. Project teams should not, however, be quick to assume that unlikely pairings of interviewer and interviewee will result in an ineffective encounter. Young people, for example, often conduct highly effective interviews with elders because they may be genuinely curious about how things used to be, long before they were born, in days they've only read about in history books. Martha Ross, an early leader in the Oral History Association, used to tell graduate students in her oral history seminars that grandchildren made great interviewers of grandparents—because they shared a common enemy.

Age differences are only one possible consideration in pairing interviewers and interviewees. Differences in race, ethnicity, religion, gender, educational background, social status, and accumulated life experiences can prove to be plusses or minuses in interviews, depending entirely on the attitudes with which both players approach the setting. An African-American college student who interviews an African-American veteran of the civil rights movement might come away with a very different interview than one conducted by a middle-aged, white accountant. A part-time waiter volunteering as an interviewer for your project might find it challenging to interview a retired insurance company executive—just as the company executive might find it challenging to interview a retired waiter. Likewise, a Baptist preacher might find it tough to interview a pro-choice advocate. And a college professor might be hard-pressed to interview a rival faculty member.

Bridging Racial Gaps

In a community oral history project that was attempting to document experiences of early African-American residents in an overwhelmingly white community, a young white woman interviewer perceived that the older African-American woman she was interviewing, and whom she deeply respected, seemed reluctant to go beyond the most superficial answers to questions about her childhood experiences. In a follow-up session, the interviewer acknowledged to her interviewee that talking about racism to a white person might be awkward or difficult, but that the older woman's experiences were important for everyone to hear about and she hoped they could at least try to address issues of racial discrimination early in the city's history. The result? The interviewee became much more forthcoming in answering questions about the town's racial climate during her childhood.

Would the interview have been different if a young African-American woman had been the interviewer? No doubt it would have been. But the white woman's respect for her interviewee and her willingness to confront openly the challenge of racial viewpoints contributed ultimately to greater candor by the interviewee.

So what is an oral history project team to do with all of these cultural variables? Stay focused on the purpose of your project. You're not matchmaking for any purpose other than conducting an oral history interview. You probably don't want your pairs to be best friends or relatives, or even people who are already well acquainted with each other. Such pairings often lead to casual conversations rather than a focused interview, and people who know each other well often are either reluctant to ask probing follow-up questions or else they speak in a shorthand that provides insufficient context for outsiders to understand. An oral history interview, after all, is a situation in which it is both appropriate and necessary to ask questions that might seem out of place in a casual conversation but that are essential nonetheless for ferreting out important details about the subject at hand.

Finally, understand the importance of training workshops addressing issues related to cross-cultural communications in the broadest sense. Interviewers who have been appropriately trained will understand that social, cultural, and personal differences may set them apart from their interviewees. They should not attempt to dismiss the importance of these differences, nor should they adopt an insincere approach to interacting with their interviewees or appear to agree with everything an interviewee says. Instead, by focusing on the mission of the oral history project and thoroughly preparing for their encounters, interviewers can bridge whatever gaps may exist between them and their interviewees and develop effective, meaningful interviews.

CHAPTER 4

Before the Interview: What Interviewers Need to Do

BEST PRACTICE NO. 2

Focus on oral history as a process.

....

BEST PRACTICE NO. 4

Understand the ethical and legal ramifications of oral history.

....

BEST PRACTICE NO. 7

Train interviewers and other project participants
to assure consistent quality.

....

Volunteers often step forward to participate in an oral history project, eagerly anticipating how much fun it will be to sit down with people and record their memories. And it is fun—but only if interviewers are well prepared. This chapter will take you through all the steps interviewers should complete before setting off for an interview. Some may be tempted to ask, You mean, I can't just go out and wing it? In a word, No. Going into an interview without proper preparation is never a good idea, and will inevitably result in an interview that's less complete than it would have been if the interviewer had done his homework ahead of time.

Here are the steps to take to make sure interviewers are well prepared.

✓ Familiarize yourself with the project goals.

✓ Get training on using the equipment and interviewing techniques.

✓ Conduct general background research.

✓ Conduct interviewee-specific research.

✓ Use the research and the project's mission statement to develop an interview guide, with questions and themes to pursue.

✓ Use appropriate recordkeeping forms, including a Legal Release Agreement.

✓ Schedule the interview.

✓ Arrive on time and bring everything you need.

✓ Arrange the interview setting.

This chapter discusses each of the preceding steps, and will help you get ready to turn on the recorder and begin asking questions.

Familiarize Yourself With the Project Goals

If you're in on the ground floor of your community oral history project, this step won't be a problem. You'll already be familiar with why the project got started, who is involved, the project's mission statement or focus, its timetable for completion, and any immediate goals to use the oral history materials in a public setting. It's critical for interviewers to understand this background, particularly the mission statement, which sets out the project's parameters. If, for example, the project focuses on a community's response to a natural disaster of historic proportions, such as a blizzard, flood, tornado, wildfire, or hurricane, the theme of the interview questions will relate to interviewees' experiences in connection with the event in question. Many of the people you interview may have other interesting life stories or experiences that people might find important and worthwhile to know. But for purposes of this project the interviews will focus solely on the event articulated in the mission statement. Interviewers need to have this firmly in mind, or else interviews can wander all over the landscape, straying far from the original purpose of the project.

Keep Interviews Focused On the Subject At Hand

Oral history interviewers will sometimes encounter interviewees who can speak articulately about the particular focus of a project but who also have compelling life stories or involvement in other aspects of the community's history that would be interesting to record. By all means, make a note of that. Interviewers could write a short summary of the additional topics about which a particular interviewee is able to share and make that part of the file on that interviewee, but interviewers generally should not veer off into asking questions during the interview about completely unrelated topics. Oral history projects have a way of spawning other oral history projects, and knowing that particular interviewees might be sources of information on additional topics could provide a useful starting point for another community history undertaking.

Get Training on Using Equipment and Interviewing Techniques

As outlined in Chapter 3, the project team should schedule appropriate training sessions for everyone who will be involved in the project. That way, all the players will clearly understand what oral history is, what the project is trying to accomplish, and what their roles will be.

As the sample training workshop agenda in Chapter 3 indicates, workshops should allow plenty of time for participants to get hands-on practice with whatever recording equipment project the project team has decided to use. (See **Volume 2,** *Planning a Community Oral History Project,* for information on selecting recording equipment and **Volume 3,** *Managing a Community Oral History Project,* for a sample equipment workshop.) Even the most technologically adept interviewers should work with the equipment until they are completely familiar with its use. How close does the microphone need to be to pick up the interviewee's and interviewer's voices? Does the interviewer need to use her reading glasses to operate the recorder's controls? Is there something quirky about how the power cord attaches? Where in the user manual does it explain how to remove the disc on which you're recording? Sitting down with your first interviewee is not the time to discover that you don't quite know how to attach the microphone to the recorder.

Be prepared to troubleshoot everything.

One oral history interviewer simply could not get her recorder to work. She got all kinds of advice to check this setting and that setting and to be sure the microphone had batteries. The problem? A faulty cord connecting the mic and the recorder. Be prepared to troubleshoot all of your equipment. And it's always best to learn how to do that in a training workshop. You'll find a sample outline for equipment training in **Volume 3,** *Managing a Community Oral History Project.*

An ability to use the equipment with confidence is an important element in establishing a positive, professional atmosphere when you get to the interview. Fumbling with the equipment only serves to draw attention to it, which tends to make interviewees ill at ease. Instead of the interviewee being the focus of the interview, the tools of the interview take center stage, and that's not where they belong.

Practice, Practice, Practice

The adage that practice makes perfect certainly applies to learning how to use oral history recording equipment. Project directors should make sure they have access to sufficient recording devices to accommodate the number of volunteer interviewers and the number of interviews planned. Interviewers need a chance to practice and practice some more before they schedule their first interview. One experienced oral historian used to tell community workshops that she liked to practice with her equipment by interviewing her cat.

Remember that a recording device will only hold a certain amount of data. Oral history interviews should be recorded in open source, uncompressed or unreconstructed digital format, known as .wav or .aiff files for audio. Standards for recording video interviews are evolving, but current practice recommends using high definition formats for recording. *Toolkit* **Volumes 2 and 3** discuss equipment in detail. Recording in uncompressed file formats allows for the most stable, long-term quality and access. But it also means you're creating very large files, so you need to know how to identify how much time is left on your recording media. You'll also need to know how to remove the disc, insert another one, and make sure the disc is functioning properly. The instruction manual that comes with your recorder should help you with these technical matters.

In addition to providing ample time to understand the equipment a project plans to use, training sessions also need to review in detail how to structure an interview and how to ask the kinds of questions that will yield full and thoughtful responses. Again, opportunities to practice these skills will prove invaluable as interviewers go into the field. Chapter 5 discusses interviewing skills in detail. Often, volunteer interviewers are themselves players in the community whose history a project is attempting to document. If they are likely to be prospective interviewees as well, it can be useful for another interviewer to practice his skills with them. The experience of being interviewed can also help an interviewer understand the process and be sensitive to the pitfalls she might encounter on the other side of the microphone.

Experienced Interviewers Need Oral History Training Too

Oral history projects occasionally will attract a volunteer whose professional background is in journalism or some other occupation that involves interviewing. That's great. But everyone involved the project, even people who think they already know how to record interviews, should be required to attend training. First, they may not know the background and focus of this particular project, and second, they may not fully understand the distinctions between oral history interviewing and whatever other kind of interviewing to which they are accustomed.

Conduct General Background Research

Ideally, the project team will have pulled together a basic reading list or lending library of background materials about the project's focus. Interviewers may be asked to be part of this task. But whether the assignment is to help identify materials or merely become familiar with materials others have gathered, getting a solid foundation in understanding what's already known about the project's topic is critical to building strong interviews. Even interviewers who have first-hand information about the subject should spend time reviewing the general background materials. They're almost certain to learn something new or be reminded of something they hadn't thought of for years. And that background is fundamental to understanding the context of an interviewee's contribution. See Chapter 3 for a complete discussion of this phase of interview preparation.

Learning the Right Vocabulary Helps Interviewers

Sometimes the most important part of reviewing general background information is becoming familiar with jargon or vocabulary unique to the subject at hand, including names of people, places, and events, which almost certainly will figure prominently in the interviews. An interviewee who stumbles in trying to recall specific terminology will appreciate an interviewer who can supply the correct word. But an interviewer who seems not to know what her interviewee is talking about will find it difficult to establish and maintain rapport and impossible to ask appropriate follow-up questions.

In one oral history project, students in a rural community's high school were paired with elderly residents of an area nursing home to conduct interviews about experiences during the Great Depression. But the students' background research was limited, and when the elders referred to the county poor farm, which housed indigent county residents in the days before government social welfare programs evolved, the students were stumped when it came to thinking of anything more to ask. The poor farm had long since been closed, and the high school students had no idea what the nursing home residents were talking about, making it impossible for them to pursue thoughtful follow-up questions.

Conduct Interviewee-Specific Research

Now we're closing in on that first oral history interview encounter. Just as it's important to understand the big picture about your topic, it's also critical to get basic background information about the individual interviewee. What is that person's connection to the subject at hand? What firsthand experiences is she in a position to relate? What is he not in a position to talk about firsthand? Knowing basic biographical information about the interviewee is a key step toward creating a successful interview.

If the interviewee is a relatively prominent person in the community, you'll probably be able to find considerable information on record about him from newspaper articles and other published accounts. If she is an author, you may not have time to read all her books, but it's a good idea to be familiar with what she's written. Local historical societies or high school yearbooks are also among the disparate sources to which you can turn for interviewee-specific background information.

Don't quiz an interviewee's friends and family as background research.

It's generally not a good idea to quiz a prospective interviewee's neighbors, relatives, or coworkers as a way to conduct interviewee-specific background research. Such actions can easily be misinterpreted as collecting idle gossip or conducting a security check, and neither of these is conducive to establishing a positive relationship with the interviewee.

Some projects take the approach of collecting background information by simply calling the interviewee and filling out the Interviewee Biographical Profile the project has established. This can be done after the interviewee has received a letter describing the project and inviting her participation, as outlined in Chapter 3. The assigned interviewer can collect the basic data in a telephone call following up on the letter and may, in the process, collect some additional background information she can further pursue in preparing for the interview. Instead of relying on the telephone, however, some projects encourage interviewers to visit a prospective interviewee in person to gather such information and answer questions about the project. A personal visit to an interviewee's home also can help an interviewer determine the best location for the interview and whether there are any distractions to work around. But pre-interview visits take time, so whether project teams choose this approach will probably depend in part on interviewer availability as well as the timeline for completing the project.

Occasionally, people will volunteer for a project who have considerable personal knowledge about interviewees' backgrounds and involvement in the subject at hand but who do not want to become project interviewers. Such volunteers, however, could be useful interview partners or helpers, working with interviewers in developing questions and providing interviewee-specific background information (see Figure 4.1 on the following page), and should be recognized as a special category of volunteers.

Develop Interview Guide with Questions and Themes to Pursue

The project's mission statement, which sets the parameters of the interviews, and the background research you've conducted will now help you craft a specific interview outline for each interviewee. An oral history interview usually unfolds in chronological order and is structured to elicit both the interviewee's information about the experiences the interview is documenting and her analysis of the information.

INTERVIEWEE BIOGRAPHICAL PROFILE	
PROJECT NAME	
Jazz Atlanta Oral History Project	
NAME	**CONTACT**
Joseph A. Browne	Atlanta Jazz Festival 246 Peach Street Atlanta, Georgia 30310 404-555-2222, x. 1 jb@aol.com
OTHER NAMES KNOWN BY	**DATE/PLACE OF BIRTH**
Joey Browne	New York, New York April 17, 1955
PLACE OF RESIDENCE	**YEARS IN THE COMMUNITY**
123 Elm Street Atlanta, Georgia 30301 404-555-111	Mr. Browne has lived in Atlanta since moving to the city to work for the Atlanta Jazz Festival in 1997.
OCCUPATION	**EDUCATION**
Jazz musician, arts administrator	Mr. Browne graduated from the New York School of the Performing Arts in 1973 and from the Tisch School of the Arts at New York University (NYU) in 1978. He received his MFA (Master of Fine Arts) from NYU in 1983. He is a jazz percussionist and has studied with Forestorn "Chico" Hamilton.
RELEVANCE TO THE PROJECT	
Mr. Browne is a jazz musician and the director of the Atlanta Jazz Festival. In addition to his administrative duties, he regularly performs in Atlanta and New Orleans jazz clubs.	
RELEVANT BIOGRAPHICAL INFORMATION **(AS IT RELATES TO THE GOALS OF THE PROJECT)**	
FAMILY (full name, date of birth, relationship to interviewee) Jane Winter, wife Date of birth: August 10, 1960 Jane Winter met the interviewee at NYU; they married 1983. She originally was from Atlanta, but had lived in New York City while attending the university. Ms. Winter is a professor of history at Georgia State University.	

Figure 4.1. Sample—Interviewee Biographical Profile *(Continued on following page)*

Figure 4.1. Sample—Interviewee Biological Profile *(continued)*

FRIENDS AND ASSOCIATES (full name, date of birth, relationship to interviewee) Mr. Browne knows most of the jazz musicians in the American South; many serve or have served on the Atlanta Jazz Festival Board of Directors.	

PLACES TRAVELED OR LIVED

Mr. Browne regularly travels to New Orleans to perform as well as to New York City several times a year when his schedule allows to perform at Jazz at Lincoln Center.

COMMUNITY ACTIVITIES (Include activity, date, and significance to the project)

Mr. Browne is very involved with the jazz community in Atlanta and in jazz communities throughout the American South. He teaches one class a year at University of Georgia and is in demand as a performer.

INTERESTS

In addition to performing and arts administration, Mr. Browne is interested in the history of jazz in the American South.

INFLUENCES

Mr. Browne's musical influences are his teachers and mentors, especially Forestorn "Chico" Hamilton. His administrative influences are his Atlanta Jazz Festival Board of Directors.

LIFE MILESTONES

In 2009, Mr. Browne was given a state arts award by the Georgia State Arts Council.

Completed by Lane Smith, Interviewer	**Date** *(insert date)*

Here is a skeleton format of what an interview outline should look like.

✓ Begin with a recorded introduction that follows a standard format.

✓ Ask for a brief personal background.

✓ Ask how the interviewee first became involved with the subject at hand.

✓ Ask follow-up questions as the interviewee's account evolves.

✓ Ask the interviewee to assess her experiences related to the event or subject of the interview.

The next several pages will put meat on these bones.

Begin With a Recorded Introduction that Follows a Standard Format

Project teams should develop specific wording for a standard introduction that should come at the beginning of each interview and should include the time, place, and purpose of the interview as well as the names of the interviewer, interviewee, and, in special circumstances, any other participants, such as an interpreter.

Sample Interview Introduction

The following interview is being conducted with
___(name of interviewee)___ for the
___(name of oral history project).___
It is taking place on ___(date)___ at
___(place).___ The interviewer is
___(name).___

The standard introduction serves several purposes. First, it clues the interviewee that the preliminary chatting you have engaged in while setting up the equipment is over and that the formal interview is about to begin. Second, it provides what amounts to an initial audio label that documents the recording.

Ask for a Brief Personal Background

Starting the interview this way usually gets things going smoothly. Most people can easily talk about themselves, and some will tell you more than you even wanted to know. But that's OK. Biographical information is important because it helps provide context to the subsequent information the interviewee will relate.

Ask How the Interviewee First Became Involved With the Subject at Hand

This question sets the stage for the bulk of the interview. Asking about the interviewee's first connection with the event or place or experience you're trying to document helps create a chronological structure, which matches how people often recount their experiences anyway.

Ask Follow-Up Questions as the Interviewee's Account Evolves

Sometimes the only prompting an interviewee will need to elaborate the story is simply the question, "And then what happened?"

One Man's Personal Background

Here's what interviewee Arne Larsen told an interviewer for the Tod's Point oral history project in Greenwich, CT, when asked for his personal background.

> "I was born in 1895 in Vega, Norway, the north part of Norway. I met my wife in Bergen, Norway, and then we left the same year we got married. I came to this country in 1919 to Norge, Virginia, near Williamsburg. In '22 I came to Greenwich, and I started work right away for the Tod family. I had a brother that worked as Mr. Tod's valet for a short time, so that's how I got up here. And since that time I lived there many years." [7]

Specific question-asking techniques are covered in detail in Chapter 5, but the important thing to remember when you put together an interview outline is to include a list of specific themes or topics you want to ask the interviewee about, based on the overall focus of the oral history project. You'll want to be sure to cover all of them during the interview. Sometimes, in talking about the topic or theme you ask about first, an interviewee will skip to another topic on your list. This may introduce it in a different order than what appears on your list, but that's OK. You can pursue follow-up questions until that topic has been covered and then go back to whatever additional topics you still need to address.

Good Follow-Up Questions Enrich Interviews

Student Tammy Caudill of Rocky Gap High School in Bland County, VA, interviewed Ora Gray Stowers about her memories of teaching in a one-room school house near Bland in 1934. The student enriched the interview by asking a good follow-up question.

Ora Gray: *School day began early. It usually began around 8:30 or even at 8:00 in the morning. School lasted until 4:00 in the afternoon. There was a mid morning recess of about ten minutes when they could go to the restrooms, usually the out door type was available. Of course, they could play and take a*

(Continued on following page)

run around the building for a little exercise and get some fresh air. Then they returned back to class until about 12. At that time they usually had an hour for their lunch period. By the time they ate their lunch if the weather was pretty and the sun was shining, they would take their lunch outside and have their lunch picnic style. Then they would play their favorite games tap hands and drop the hankie. The boys liked to play baseball. Some of the old fashioned games like paddle ball were common also. In the winter if there was a small hillside by the boys, one would bring a nice big sled and the teachers and students would sleigh ride down the hill. That was a favorite in the winter. When school started back, a teacher would stand at the door and [ring] a bell so the children would go back to their classes. Then at 2:00 P.M., there was a ten minute break so the students could go to the restroom, get a drink of water, or go outside and play.

Tammy: *Ok, that drop the hankie. What was involved with it? What was involved with tap the hand?*

Ora Gray: *To play drop the hankie, the children stood in a circle and held hands. One student took the hankie on the outside of the circle and dropped it behind someone. You had to be alert and watch for the hankie, so you could let loose of the other students' hands so you could pick up the hankie. When you got the hankie, you ran after the person who dropped it behind you. If you could catch him, then he had to go around the second time. If you couldn't catch him, then you had to take the hankie and continue the game. Tap the hand was about the same but no hankie was used. You tapped the person on the hand or the arm and the chase began.[7]*

In addition to listing on the interview outline the specific topics you plan to pursue, interviewers also find it useful to include specific dates, names, or other information that might help when an interviewee struggles to remember such details.

Resist the temptation to write out questions word for word. Just make a list of key words or phrases or specific topics you need to pursue. Interviewers who write out complete questions have a tendency to read them like a script, much like one of those telemarketers who call at dinnertime. This stilted approach does not lend itself to the comfortable, natural flow an oral history interview should reflect.

Ask the Interviewee to Assess Her Experiences

Questions that encourage interviewees to reflect on their experiences can yield the personal insights that distinguish oral history from other kinds of historical research. Why does the interviewee think things happened the way they did? What did she think about it at the time? What does she think about it now? People often reinterpret their own experiences in the light of new experiences, and oral history interviews allow you to capture that reassessment, leading to a fuller understanding of the meaning and significance of the subject at hand. Asking for this kind of analysis and reflection also clues the interviewee that the interview is winding down and allows for a graceful conclusion to the interview session.

What an Interview Outline Looks Like

Here's an example of how the skeleton interview outline looks when fleshed out for a specific project. The Obama Volunteers Story Project was undertaken by researchers Cyns Nelson and Steve Kennedy in an attempt to document the experiences of Colorado volunteers who worked on the presidential campaign of Barack Obama in 2008.[8]

Interview Outline for Interviewees

Where and when were you born? Comments on upbringing.

Talk about how/why you came to be involved in the Campaign for Change.

- Reflect on your personal history
- Draw connections between your past and what's happening today

Share specific stories that gave meaning to your experience.

- Where/how you participated
- Specific encounters during the campaign
- Surprises
- Feelings/emotions at different times

How have you changed because of your involvement with the campaign? What difference has this made?

Talk about what you're doing now, plans for the future, and your hopes.

In working through this discussion of developing an interview outline of questions and themes to pursue based on project research, you may wonder if there isn't an easier way. Why not just Google "oral history questions?" Surely we'll find something there. Yes, you will. You'll get hundreds of hits. You'll find a site willing to sell you a workbook of 430 questions. You'll find a site that instructs interviewers to ask about the floor plan of the family home, their mother's hairstyle and what the person recalls about the Cuban missile crisis. And you'll find instructions for asking the first question: "Please state your full name and present address."

Most of the canned lists of questions, either online or in widely varying instruction books and magazine articles, are geared for people doing genealogy research or trying to capture stories at family reunions or from older relatives in general. Whatever usefulness they have for those purposes, they certainly don't come close to helping with a community oral history project. You will not find online or in this *Toolkit* prepared lists of questions you can use because only you know what your project is trying to accomplish. The community you're setting out to study is, by definition, unique. So even though it may seem a laborious process to develop a thoroughly researched question outline for your interviewees, it's the key to successful oral history interviews.

Don't Ask Questions Like a Cop

"Please state your full name and present address." Think about how an interviewee might respond to this just-the-facts-ma'am, law-enforcement-officer question. Most interviewers will be able to think of a much friendlier-sounding way to get that information.

Use Appropriate Recordkeeping Forms

At this stage in preparing for the interview, it will be helpful to make sure you have all the appropriate recordkeeping forms in place. For most projects, this will include an Interviewee Biographical Profile and an Interview Summary, which you will use to document details of the interview, and the Legal Release Agreement that both the interviewee and interviewer will sign at the end of the interview session. Samples of all of these forms can be found in the appendix to **Volume 1,** *Introduction to Community Oral History* and online at www.LCoastPress.com (go to *Toolkit* page)..

Schedule the Interview

If your oral history project follows the suggestions in Chapter 3 about sending introductory letters to prospective interviewees, the task of the interviewer will be to make follow-up phone calls, being prepared to answer questions about the oral history process and ready to schedule time for an interview at the interviewee's convenience.

Here are the three most important criteria to consider when setting a time and place for an oral history interview.

- *Will the interviewee be comfortable?* Many interviews take place in the interviewee's home, but sometimes small rooms are available at the local library or in some other location. Occasionally an interviewee prefers to be interviewed in his office or place of work.

- *Is the setting quiet and will the interview be undisturbed?* Sometimes homes are noisy places, with children, pets, or a collection of antique clocks that strike every 15 minutes. And sometimes offices and other work places are noisy or prone to interruptions like phone calls or visitors dropping in. You'll just have to use your judgment, but be sure to make clear to the interviewee that you'll need uninterrupted time in a quiet place so the sound quality of the recording will be as clean as you can make it.

- *Will the interviewee have sufficient time and energy to devote to the interview?* Even though it might work best for you, it's seldom a good idea to try to talk an interviewee into squeezing in an interview between other commitments. An oral history interview is not a quick, 20-minute, superficial encounter. Oral history interviews can take up to an hour and a half or so, plus set-up time, and it takes considerable mental energy to participate in such an in-depth encounter. A tired interviewee—or one who is distracted by thinking about where she has to be in an hour—is unlikely to be able to contribute in the same way she could in a more leisurely setting.

A pre-interview visit with your interviewee can be helpful in determining whether there are any conditions in the interview environment that you will need to address. Will a barking, meowing, or chirping pet be an issue? How about an in-home preschool daycare? Or a loudly vibrating window air conditioner? Does the interviewee's favorite chair emit a distracting squeak every time she rocks? Will electricity be available if you'd planned to use an external power source for your equipment? Does the interviewee have physical limitations that affect his speaking ability or require him to take frequent breaks? A pre-interview visit also will allow you to answer questions about the oral history project, the Legal Release Agreement, and any other details about how the interview materials are expected to be used, all of which will help you build rapport. Additionally, such a visit will allow you to determine just where the interview site is located and how long it will take you to get there.

A possible disadvantage of a pre-interview visit is that interviewees sometimes are so excited and ready to share their experiences that they launch into their stories even though you haven't brought your equipment, paperwork, and questions. If your project director asks interviewers to conduct pre-interview visits, try to discourage interviewees from telling their tales in that initial meeting. Given the practicalities, many projects try to accomplish most of the tasks of a pre-interview visit in the telephone call in which the interviewer schedules the interview. Pre-interview visits can add time and scheduling complications for busy volunteers, but if you don't visit ahead of the interview, plan to take enough time when you arrive for the interview to establish a positive working relationship with the interviewee and to resolve any problems that may affect the quality of the recording.

Don't Crowd an Interviewee's Schedule

University of Maryland oral history teacher Martha Ross used to get a laugh out of her graduate students when she admonished them that old people only do one thing every day: get their hair done, go to a doctor's appointment, shop for groceries, and the like. Think about your older relatives or friends, and you'll know she was right. So if your potential interviewee says she has a doctor's appointment on Tuesday morning, it's probably not wise to suggest the interview for Tuesday afternoon. Perhaps Monday or Wednesday would be better days.

Arrive on Time and Bring Everything You Need

Always arrive on time for your interview and be sure to bring along all your materials: equipment, extra pens, notebook, outline, Legal Release Agreement and any appropriate interview prompts such as old photographs or newspaper clippings. Oral history is fun, but it's also serious business, and it pays to be organized and act professional as you get acquainted with the interviewee and get the process started.

Get Clear Directions in Advance to the Interview Location

If you're going to an unfamiliar location, be sure to ask for specific directions on how to get there. Never rely on a route that an online route-finding site gives you. Such sites can provide bad advice. Unless your project can afford GPS equipment for all its volunteers, it's usually just easiest to ask the interviewee how to get to get there. If the interview is scheduled at night, try to take the time during daylight hours to make a reconnaissance trip to the location. Finding unfamiliar addresses at night can be challenging, and the last thing an interviewer wants is to get lost and arrive late, which gets the interview session off to a bad start.

Arrange the Interview Setting

Oral history project teams often assemble interviewing kits for the volunteers that include all the basic materials they'll need.

THINGS TO INCLUDE IN AN INTERVIEWING KIT

✓ recorder and its instruction manual

✓ microphone

✓ necessary power and adapter cords, including an extension cord or extra batteries

✓ earphones

✓ recording media, such as removable discs

✓ Legal Release Agreement, Interviewee Biographical Profile, and Interview Summary

✓ small camera for taking photos of the interviewee

✓ notebook and pens or pencils for jotting down notes during the interview—a steno-pad sized notebook works best

Interviewers should always carefully check the bag of basic materials be-fore setting out, just to be sure an item wasn't borrowed and not returned. In addition, you'll be adding your own folder of notes, your interview outline, and anything else you think might contribute to a rich interview. Sometimes maps, photographs, and other objects serve as props that can engage the in-terviewee and prompt memories. If those are relevant to your project, bring them along, too.

Once you arrive at the interview location—and, once again, be sure you arrive on time—the first task is to determine where the interview will take place, if this is your first visit to the location. Keep in mind the need to maxi-mize interviewee comfort and minimize audible background sound and in-terruptions. Unplug or otherwise silence telephones, if possible. (Remember to turn them on again before you leave.) Ask that other people—adults and children—and pets be kept out of the interview room, unless, of course, the interview includes a person who is serving as an interpreter. Turn off radios, televisions, and other sources of background music and conversation. In short, try to anticipate, to the extent possible, the kinds of audible interrup-tions that may mar the quality of your recording.

The more familiar you are with your equipment and its technical capa-bilities, the easier it will be for you to set up smoothly, without undue fuss-ing. Place your recorder on a table or some other solid surface, positioning it so that you can easily reach the controls without turning your attention away from the interviewee. The two of you should be able to make direct eye contact without turning to one side or the other. The microphone likewise should be placed close enough to both of you to record both voices (see Figure 4.2). If your project is using clip-on microphones, be sure neither you nor the interviewee is wearing scarves or jewelry that could yield a rustling or clinking sound when the speaker turns her head or shifts in her chair.

If your project is video recording the interviews, you'll be guided by whatever specific arrangements your project has made. Sometimes a volun-teer will be assigned specifically to deal with the equipment; in other cases, the interviewer will be expected to set up and monitor the equipment as well as conduct the interview. Some projects may need to use auxiliary lights; others will use equipment for which ambient light is sufficient.

In any case, the set-up for a video-recorded interview is similar to that for an audio-recorded interview. The interviewee and interviewer should be comfortable, and the equipment should not create an intrusion. The cam-era should be positioned over the interviewer's shoulder so it can focus ex-clusively on the interviewee. Use a standard head-and-shoulders shot, with the interviewee comfortably framed with enough space above her head and

Figure 4.2. Henry E. Frye, former North Carolina Supreme Court chief justice, is interviewed by Katherine Otis of the Southern Oral History Program, University of North Carolina at Chapel Hill. The photo illustrates an appropriate way to set up an oral history interview in a quiet location without interruption. The interviewer is positioned so she can make eye contact with the interviewee but also keep an eye on the recorder. The external microphone is positioned to pick up both voices, and the interviewer has a notepad to keep track of follow-up questions.
Photo credit: Southern Oral History Program

in front of her face so the image isn't tightly cropped. Frame the shot with enough room to allow for casual movement within the frame, so when the interviewee shifts positions in his chair, he doesn't move out of the picture. Also check to be sure there isn't a picture frame, floor lamp, or potted plant that appears to be growing out of the interviewee's head. Busy backgrounds are best avoided, as is busy clothing. Consider asking the interviewee in advance not to wear a plaid, striped, or polka-dotted top. Also, plain white shirts can cause glare in a video setting, and wildly colorful scarves or neckties can be distracting.

If your project is using video to document a particular visual aspect of the community, or if you know the interview will have an important visual element, documenting that visual component sometimes can be done in a separate session. Perhaps you'll want to conduct an audio-only oral history interview and then make additional arrangements to video-record a tour of the neighborhood or the historic barn or the unique artifact collection. In other words, don't try to do everything at once.

If it makes things easier, audio- and video-recordings can be made at different times.

The interview itself deserves the complete attention of both interviewer and interviewee, as does the effort to visually document the important elements of the project. Some oral historians have found it useful to go back for a second interview, this time on video, in which the interviewee takes the interviewer to the place that figures into the story. The interviewee then can repeat, on camera, the information about that place. Again, be flexible, but keep in mind your project's mission, your interviewee's availability, and the goal of achieving the cleanest recording possible, both visually and audibly, to maximize future use of the material.

Remember that in a video-recorded oral history interview, you're not creating a Ken Burns documentary or an MTV video. Forget the special effects: no zooming, no panning, no unflattering camera angles, and no switching between the interviewer and interviewee. The interviewer should be on camera to state the introduction and to put a face to the voice asking questions. But after that, the camera should be repositioned to focus exclusively on the interviewee.

Keep in mind that you're creating raw materials for your project and other historians after you to use. If you video record oral history interviews, they shouldn't look like a produced TV documentary. The false starts, the interviewee's pauses to collect herself, the awkward request to repeat a question— all of those could be edited out in a polished video presentation. So don't imagine yourself conducting an interview segment for the evening news. You're creating primary sources that historians of tomorrow may treasure.

CHAPTER 5

During the Interview

BEST PRACTICE NO. 8

Conduct interviews that will stand the test of time.

Now you're ready for your oral history interview. All your preparations so far—planning, research, training workshops, equipment practice, and everything else—will contribute to the success of the interview you're about to begin.

You've set up your equipment—either audio or video and with or without equipment helpers—and now you need to perform an equipment check to make sure everything is in working order so that you'll record both the interviewee's voice and your own. Remember that an oral history interview is the product of an exchange between two people. Some forms of recorded information gathering, like what folklorists do, for example, focus primarily on documenting what the interview subject says or does. In the case of folklore, that might mean recording someone performing traditional songs or using traditional instruments or reciting traditional stories. An oral history, on the other hand, is created when a well-prepared oral historian asks specific questions of an interviewee, who then responds. That exchange, the two-way communication, creates an oral history interview. In other words, we want to know what question you asked that elicited the interviewee's particular response. So when you do your sound check, be sure you can hear both voices well. Adjust the recording levels or reposition the microphone, so you know you'll get it all. It's best not to make a big production of this because it can make some interviewees nervous. Just ask your interviewee to say her name or recite something innocuous—a list of numbers, a nursery rhyme—so you can accommodate your equipment settings to her normal speaking voice.

Help Your Interviewee Relax and Stay Focused

Oral historians occasionally encounter an interviewee who is quite chatty but who clams up as soon as the recorder is turned on. If that happens, just remind the person that you're not creating a polished final product and that it's OK if she doesn't speak in complete sentences and wants to start over again when articulating a particular thought. The more matter-of-fact and confident you can be as the interviewer, the more you'll help your interviewee relax and focus on articulating her memories.

After you've tweaked the recording set-up, make sure you and your interviewee are comfortable. Having to twist awkwardly in a chair to speak into the microphone will be tiring and will not lend itself to a relaxed, productive interview for either one of you. You'll especially want to be sure you are positioned to monitor your recording equipment throughout the interview to make sure no problems develop. If at any point you detect that something has gone wrong with recording the voices, don't hesitate to stop, check everything out, and then pick up where you left off. It might seem awkward, but it's in everyone's interest to make sure the recording process works well. Your interviewee will understand.

Often, your interviewee will offer you refreshments, perhaps mistakenly perceiving this one-on-one exchange as a social event. Politely decline such offers until the interview is over. The clinking of tea cups and coffee mugs or forks on a pie plate will mar the recording. (But don't hesitate to say you'll accept that piece of pie after the interview, if it seems appropriate.) Depending on the circumstances, it is often a good idea, however, to bring along small bottles of water for you and your interviewee. Long-winded interviewees will appreciate a quick sip of water from time to time, and this is usually not disruptive on the recording.

Next, it's time for you to record the standard introduction your project is using. Here's what it might look like.

This is an interview with Pastor Adam Smith of the Dutch Reformed Lutheran Church in Dinsmore County for the History of Dinsmore County Oral History Project. The interview is taking place at Pastor Smith's parsonage on August 6, 2012. The interviewer is Kay Alexander.

As noted in the earlier discussion about developing an interview guide, a recorded introduction begins the process of creating documentation for the interview. Future users will know from the recording itself whose voices are on the recording as well as when, where and why it took place. To that end, if your interview involves a translator or other assistant, be sure to include that person's name and identification in the recorded introduction. Note also that the introduction need not include a statement of what topics the interview will cover. Doing so might suggest to the interviewee that you're only interested in those items and not interested in hearing anything else, even though it could lead to important new information for the project.

Introducing a Follow-Up Interview

An exception to the general rule of not listing topics for discussion would be a circumstance in which you're conducting a follow-up interview. In that case, you might state the standard introduction, adding that it's a second (or third or whatever) interview with the person. Then preface the questions themselves by saying, for example, "We talked earlier about the founding of this congregation, and today I'd like to focus on how you started the school." Indeed, life interviews, in which the same person is interviewed multiple times in an effort to document that person's entire life or career, would generally include an opening focus statement as one way to help both interviewee and interviewer keep on track. But again, it's important not to let that focus become a limiting factor as the interview unfolds.

Asking the Questions

The interview guide, or topic outline, that you developed based on your research now becomes your blueprint from which to build your interview. This section will suggest a variety of effective question-asking strategies, but interviewers should keep in mind two overarching ethical tenets.

First, an oral history interview creates a new primary source of information about a specific time and place in the past—either distant or recent. And it will have an important advantage over other kinds of primary documents, like transcripts of government meetings or personal diaries, because you, the interviewer, have a chance to probe more deeply into the source's statements. You can pin down details that are missing from diary accounts and inquire why your interviewee did what he did or why she thinks things worked out the way they did. Indeed, that ability to go beneath the surface or beyond the accepted public view of events is why we do oral history in the first place.

Second, interviewees are always entitled to respect for their views, even if they strike you as utterly ridiculous or improbable. An oral history interview is not the time or place to argue over personal opinions.

 Clarify and probe, but don't argue over personal opinions.

But by all means, ask probing follow-up questions to flesh out your interviewee's views or clarify information that conflicts with other versions of events already on the record. You may not be able to resolve discrepancies, but you've done your job by exploring them. And in some cases, even the discrepancies can give you important insights.

The Value of Something That Couldn't be True

Sometimes oral historians will encounter a situation in which an interviewee describes something that the person couldn't possibly know about firsthand. Take, for example, the case of an elderly woman who recalled seeing Charles Lindbergh when he stopped in Nebraska, where he had learned to fly, on a nationwide tour following his nonstop trans-Atlantic flight. Other family members, however, asserted unequivocally that the woman was nowhere near Nebraska at the time Lindbergh was touring.

So what are we to make of that? Is the woman making it up? Misremembering? Or is the family lying?

While it might or might not be important to try to pin down the facts in such a case, even more important is understanding that the Lindbergh flight and his subsequent national tour was such a dramatic event of the day that the woman somehow needed to associate herself with it. In other words, we learn more about the significance of the event than we do about the facts—or non-facts—of her experiences and thus have a better appreciation for the dramatic impact of Lindbergh's historic flight.

Some oral historians suggest that interviewers should strike a conversational tone to put the interviewee at ease in asking questions. A conversational style is certainly better than an adversarial one, but beware of falling into a conversational trap. Many people don't pay close attention to exactly how they speak in the course of everyday conversation. Often, everyday discourse would be pretty ineffective as an interviewing style. Indeed, an oral history interview often is described as an opportunity to ask the kinds of probing questions that might be considered impolite or out of place in a typical conversational setting. So an oral history interviewer needs to be acutely aware of how to phrase questions to elicit the most effective, complete responses.

Ask Open-Ended, Neutral Questions, Rather than Closed Questions or Leading Questions

Labor historian Alice Hoffman, an early leader in the Oral History Association, often pointed out that within every question is embedded an expected response. For example, if a questioner says: "Did you like your new job?" there is an implied "yes" or "no." What if the person thought it was OK some days but not others? In any case, the question is not likely to take you beyond a simple answer. What if you asked, "How did you like your new job?" This question itself still presumes "likingness." It would be more neutral, and thus better, to ask, "Tell me about your new job." Note, it's not "Can you tell me about your new job?" as that takes us back to the beginning, inviting a simple yes-no response.

Asking Open-Ended Questions

Here's an easy way to think about open-ended inquiries. Questions that begin with *who, what, where, when, why, how* and *tell me about…* will almost always lead to longer, descriptive answers than questions beginning with *can, did, would* or *could*.

Certainly you will want to ask narrow, pointed questions from time to time to pin down specific information, as in, for example, How many children attended that one-room school? And often, you'll want to pin down specific names, dates or other such details. But the goal in an oral history interview is to elicit detailed responses to broadly worded questions, not a staccato back-and-forth that might be typical of a prosecuting attorney's cross-examination of a defense witness.

Be an Active Listener So You'll Know When to Ask Follow-Up Questions

This is harder than it sounds. If you've done appropriate background research, you'll know when you're hearing something new or at odds with what's already on the record. Those are the details you should pursue. Often, your follow-up question will be as simple as saying: "Tell me more about that" or "Describe that day for me."

Setting Up Questions

Some oral historians suggest crafting questions in the form of two sentences, in which the first sentence draws on your background research or something the interviewee has already said as a way to set the stage for a topic of discussion. Here's an example.

> I understand that you were just 18 years old when you got your teaching certificate and started in the country school. What was it like when you first stood up in front of your class?

Referring to your own background research in that way can be an effective way to establish rapport with your interviewee; she will know you've cared enough to do your homework. But be careful not to go on and on showing off how much you know. The interviewee is likely to wonder why you bothered to talk to him if you already know everything.

Don't Walk Away From Controversial Topics

An oral history project is an opportunity to explore all sides of an issue, and sometimes a project may deal with struggles a community has not yet resolved. In such cases, an oral history project can be a neutral meeting ground for people with widely varying and fervently held points of view to document their experiences with the controversy. It sometimes can be hard for interviewers to ask questions about a topic, when they know the answers are going to reflect emotional or strongly held positions. It also can be hard to ask questions about something you feel strongly about. That's when careful attention to wording questions neutrally can be an effective way to generate important new information.

Choosing the Best Approach to Controversial Questions

Look at the differences in how an interviewer might phrase questions about the city's plans to demolish a neighborhood for a new freeway interchange.

> *So were you really mad when you got the letter saying your house was in the freeway path?*

Versus

> *Tell me your reaction when you got the letter saying your house was in the freeway path.*

> *I gather that people in this neighborhood don't really believe the city officials' explanation for why we need this road. Is that about right?*

Versus

> *City officials have been quoted as saying the road will be an economic boost to the neighborhood. What's your view of that?*

Also keep in mind that an oral historian's role is to ask questions, not engage in debates with the interviewees. But you should not passively take at face value an interviewee's statements that seem sharply at odds with information already on the record about a particular topic. A useful way to ask probing follow-up questions in such circumstances is to phrase them as a devil's advocate.

Playing the Devil's Advocate

Here's how a question might be phrased with the interviewer playing devil's advocate.

> *So, you say the party activists needed to take control of the county political conventions. What would be your response to those who argue that the conventions have become a way to make back-room deals?*

Ask One Question at a Time and Then Stop Talking

Resist the temptation to string multiple questions together, as one might do in casual conversation. Such smorgasbord questions look like this.

> *What was it like when you first moved to the farm, were there chores to do, did it seem awfully quiet after living in the city, how long did it take you to get used to that country school?*

Savvy politicians faced with such a string of questions will sometimes attempt to insult the reporter who asked it by saying, "So which question did you want me to answer?" Your oral history interviewee, on the other hand, is likely just to be confused. Certainly you'll want to explore all those ideas, but if you ask this kind of question, your interviewee won't know where to begin. Moreover, such an approach violates the rule discussed earlier in that the question presumes a range of specific answers.

Silence is Golden

If you ask a question that is met initially by silence, resist the temptation to jump in and start augmenting the question or attempting to clarify it. Your interviewee may simply be gathering his thoughts and formulating his response. Give him time to do so without further chatter. Similarly, when an interviewee finishes answering a question, wait a moment before jumping in with your next question. She might add more information if you let a few moments of silence ensue, along with an interested and expectant facial expression.

In most social circumstances where conversation is going on, people generally abhor silence and will jump in to fill it. Use that phenomenon to your advantage. Instead of being the person filling the silence with unnecessary additions to your question, just be patient and see how the interviewee responds.

Startling Information Can Emerge

Occasionally, an interviewee will reveal something startling in the course of answering an otherwise innocuous question. That's what happened in an interview with Minnesota newspaper editor Alan T. Zdon, in an oral history project about Minnesota Governor Rudy Perpich. Interviewer Barbara W. Sommer asked Zdon to describe the former governor's family.

Zdon: *I know them because I met them a dozen times or so over the years. We didn't ever sit down and play cards and have conversations or things like that. His mother is very quiet when*

I was around. I never saw her in the family setting. His dad was friendly to me and you could talk to his dad and engage him in a conversation. Very proud of Rudy. They both were. They were very solid people, is kind of the way I thought of them. They were very rugged and had, obviously, gone through a lot. And they had raised these four boys. I guess I am going to tell you something that I don't know if you have gotten from anybody else. Especially when you talk about Rudy's parents and Rudy's mom, this is kind of a family secret of sorts. Rudy told me in confidence at one time. But I think it should be part of the historical record. There was a baby girl in the family. Mrs. Perpich was canning and she had heated up a large washtub of boiling water. That was also the washtub where the kids bathed. So, the little girl, without even thinking, thought it was bath time and jumped in the water and scalded herself to death. That had a tremendous, traumatic effect on Rudy's mom that she never overcame. To this day, the family never mentions that there was a girl in the family. I have never heard it mentioned anywhere at any time in any biography or anything like that. But there was. I think that whole episode had a very deep, deep effect on that family—to lose their baby sister like that. You can imagine, after, I don't know where she fit in, except that she was younger than, I think, the three older boys. She may have been somewhere around the time of Joe.

Sommer: *Sad thing to happen.*

Zdon: *That was back in Carson Lake, when that happened.*

Sommer: *That is really sad. His parents didn't ever say anything to you about it, or his brothers? Just Rudy?*

Zdon: *Yes. Rudy is the only one who ever talked about it.*[10]

Don't Interrupt

This is something your mother might have taught you. In an oral history interview, interrupting is not only impolite, but it also can disrupt the interviewee's train of thought and prevent him from developing the idea he's trying to express. Resist the temptation to interrupt, even if the interviewee's answer to your question seems to go far afield. That's just the way some people talk about their memories—you ask them what time it is and they tell you how to make a watch.

When this happens, it's often because the interviewee believes you need to understand more background so the context of her story will become clear. Let her talk. It may seem like rambling, but be willing to take a chance that she actually might be going somewhere with her tale. If you become convinced that it's truly a ramble—perhaps she'll even say, "Now what did you ask me?"—gently steer her back on track with something like, "We were talking about the time you started a neighborhood garden in the playground."

Sometimes, an interviewee uses slang terms or professional jargon you might not be familiar with, despite your best efforts to prepare for the interview. In such circumstances, a quick interruption at the outset—as soon as the unfamiliar terminology emerges—might be the best choice, because if you don't understand it, chances are people listening to the interview later won't get it either. You could quickly interject, "Tell us what you mean by…". Another option would be to jot down the unfamiliar terms on your notepad and ask for clarification when she pauses. In any case, it's important to get that information before you leave the interview; unfamiliar terms, abbreviations or acronyms should be spelled out in a footnote in the transcript.

If I've Heard This Story Once, I've Heard It a Thousand Times

If you come from a family of storytellers, you'll be familiar with the rehearsed tale told at reunions or other gatherings by the elderly relative who uses virtually the same words with the same expressions and the same pauses for laugh lines—over and over and over again. You've heard it so often, you could recite it, too.

It's not unusual for oral historians to encounter the rehearsed story. Rather than interrupt the interviewee—he's probably telling it because he likes to hear it too—listen to the story and let him get it out of his system. Here's where your notepad comes in handy. As you listen, jot down questions that occur to you. What details is he leaving out? How did other people react to the episode? Those are the kinds of questions that can turn even a well-rehearsed tale into a nugget of new information you can draw out in an oral history interview.

Use Body Language, Not Verbal Comments, to Encourage the Interviewee

Nothing mars an otherwise great oral history interview more than an interviewer who constantly says "Uh-huh" or "I see" or "Really?" as a running backdrop to the interviewee's story. This is another example of how an oral history interview is not like a casual conversation. Many people interject audible responses while they listen as a way to let the person who is speaking know they are paying attention. But an interviewer who does that in an oral history interview has just compromised the recording so that it would be difficult or even impossible to use in a public presentation. To the extent that oral history recordings find homes in radio documentaries, museum exhibits, and online publications, a clean, clear voice with no extraneous background interruptions is essential.

So instead of saying "Uh-huh," use body language to let the interviewee know you're paying attention and are interested. Nod. Make eye contact. Smile. Look interested or curious. And when you jot down things in your notebook that you want to follow up, don't bury your nose there. Glance down long enough to write what you need and then look back up at the interviewee. Likewise, avoid being distracted by your own outline or background materials. Asking a question and then immediately shuffling through papers while the person is answering sends an unspoken message that you're not interested in what the interviewee has to say.

Making sure your materials are organized and easy to read before you start the interview can keep this from becoming a problem.

Read the Interviewee's Body Language and Vocal Cues

Experienced interviewers learn how to read subtle hints in an interviewee's demeanor. Even changes in tone of voice may suggest she has more to say on a topic or is either enthusiastic or uncomfortable with the direction an interview is going. Sometimes an interview involves emotionally laden topics that may be difficult for the interviewee to recount—and difficult for the interviewer to hear. In such cases, it's best to avoid fussing over the interviewee. But it might be appropriate to take a short break to allow the interviewee to regain her composure.

Tone of Voice Alone Can Tell Part of the Story

In one oral history project, an eighth-grade girl who was born in China but who hadn't lived there since she was a toddler, interviewed her grandmother, who was visiting the family in the United States. The interview was in Chinese. Even a listener who knew nothing of the language could tell solely from the grandmother's tone of voice on the recording when the discussion turned to a highly emotional topic. She lowered her voice, spoke in shorter, choppier sentences and sounded sad. The granddaughter explained her grandmother was recounting her experiences during China's Cultural Revolution of the 1960s and 1970s, when she and millions of others were swept up in the widespread violence and persecution of that era.

Remember That You're Not Producing a Segment for the Nightly News

Sometimes novice oral historians—and their interviewees—become concerned over false starts, pauses, re-phrases and the like in both questions and answers. Don't be. The fundamental purpose of an oral history interview is to collect new information for the historical record. It need not look or sound like a slickly produced segment from a television documentary or newscast. If your project intends to produce a documentary or feature portions of an interview on a website, elements like false starts or pauses can be edited out. What's harder to deal with from a public programming standpoint is a recording with a dog barking in the background or a video in which the changing view out a window creates a distraction. And those problems are easy to avoid if you've set up the interview appropriately in the first place.

Use Research Notes to Keep Things Moving

For many interviews, it may be useful to keep handy a list of names, dates, places, and other facts derived from the timeline your project has created. Interviewees sometimes stumble over recalling such specifics, and if you can provide the details when the interviewee draws a blank over a particular name or date, you'll be able to keep the interview moving. If the interviewee is searching his memory for a fact he cannot quite recall, and it's also one you don't know and don't have on your list, you can keep him from being frustrated and keep the interview from bogging down by saying something like, "We can look that up later and add it as a footnote to the transcript."

Watching an Interview Disintegrate

A faculty member was compiling information to write a history of his college and arranged to interview a legendary former dean who was becoming quite frail. The interviewer asked how he ended up going to graduate school. The dean went on at some length about that subject, and then the interviewer asked, "Now, when did you graduate?" The dean couldn't recall, and it is clear from reading a transcript of the session that the memory lapse really bothered him. He called out to his wife in the next room, who also apparently couldn't come up with the date immediately. The interviewer kept trying to prompt him by asking whether it was before such-and-such or after this and that, which flustered him even more. Nothing productive came out of the interview thereafter, and their session soon ended altogether.

At least two lessons can be drawn from this episode. First, do your homework and bring along appropriate background information so an interview won't bog down from an interviewee's faulty memory, and second, it's seldom necessary to ask for basic, undisputed factual information like the year a prominent person graduated from college or graduate school. That's the kind of information that almost surely is already on record and can easily be discovered. Interviewers should avoid taking up time in an oral history interview asking such questions in the first place.

Use Photos, Maps, or Other Objects as Prompts to Jog Your Interviewee's Memory

Sometimes memory-jogging prompts will be items you've brought with you, as we discussed in the previous chapter. But your interviewee also may have photos, scrapbooks, or other objects that spark stories about the topics you wish to pursue. Occasionally, the interviewee is willing to donate such items to the oral history project, and your project team should anticipate this and have a protocol for dealing with such offers. Other times, the interviewees will be willing to loan photos or scrapbooks to the project so they can be copied and made part of the collection. *Toolkit* **Volume 2,** *Planning a Community Oral History Project* and **Volume 3,** *Managing a Community Oral History Project* provide more information on these concerns.

As you talk about such items during the interview, be sure to describe them appropriately so people reading the transcript or listening to the recording can match the objects correctly to the descriptions. If your interview is being video-recorded, you can prop the items up in front of the camera while they're being discussed. But even so, it's useful to try to borrow them to make copies of the items or take photos of three-dimensional objects for the files.

Here's What a Scrapbook Page Discussion Might Look Like:

Q: *Tell me about that senior sneak when you went off to see the circus.*

A: *Well, we all took the train over to Lakeport, didn't tell our folks where we were going. One of the guys, Harvey Bloom, I believe it was, took a picture of all of us at the station. See, here's me.*

Q: *That would be the girl in the straw hat second from the left in the front row?*

A: *Yeah. And these boys were twins. Blaine and Boris Bland. Never did understand why their folks named 'em like that.*

Q: *They're the ones in matching plaid shirts in the upper right?*

Wear a Watch and Keep Track of the Time

Oral historians and their interviewees can become so engrossed in the process that they lose track of time. This is never a good idea. First, your recording device will likely have a finite number of minutes or hours it can record. Recording in standard uncompressed digital audio (.wav files) consumes considerable space on your recorder. But your device usually will have an indicator that tells you how much recording time you have left. You should keep track of it so you don't lose the tail end of an important story because your recorder has stopped. If you're using removable discs, ask the interviewee to pause briefly while you change to a new one and continue the interview with a new introduction in which you state it is "Disc 2 of the interview with Mr. Smith."

Important as it is that you make sure your recorder doesn't run out of space, it's also useful to keep track of the time, because you and your interviewee will become too tired to be effective if you let the interview run more than about an hour and a half.

Maximum interview length should be about an hour and a half.

If you're conducting life interviews where multiple sessions are scheduled, or if you know in advance you want to break up the interview time into several segments, plan to wrap things up when you get to a logical stopping place and arrange to resume at another time if you still need more information from this particular interviewee. If a project has a fairly narrow focus or if your interviewee's firsthand knowledge encompasses a fairly limited range of information, your oral history interview may cover everything in forty-five minutes to an hour.

If your interviewee turns out to be an unexpected goldmine, however, it's usually best if you can look for a good place to stop after an hour and a half or so and then ask if the interviewee can schedule another time for you to come back and finish on another day. You and your interviewee both may be tired, and it will likely make for a more effective interview if you start fresh a second time, if possible. It also will give you and your interviewee a chance to review what you've already discussed and identify what you need to cover in a second interview.

Wind Up the Interview Gracefully

If you followed the format for structuring an oral history interview that was outlined in the previous chapter, you'll see that the final phase of an interview asks the interviewee to reflect on her experiences. Why does she think things happened the way they did? What did she think of it then? What does she think of it now? These kinds of questions signal to the interviewee that the interview is winding to a close. But they also can yield important new insights about the topic at hand. People reinterpret situations and their roles over time, and understanding this can offer new perspectives about old issues.

It's also useful as you wind up to ask interviewees if you have missed anything or overlooked some aspect of the topic or if they have any other thoughts to add. This gives them an opportunity to make final comments or add information that wasn't covered or that they may have forgotten earlier. Once again, you'll just have to use your own judgment if the interviewee raises a pertinent but otherwise ignored issue. Perhaps it's a topic that can be addressed fairly quickly. But if not, you might want to schedule a second interview. It's also important to communicate new, unanticipated information to project coordinators because it may reflect an aspect of the topic that

A Graceful Interview Ending

Here's how interviewer Barbara Sommer ended the interview with newspaper editor Zdon about his involvement with Minnesota Governor Perpich:

Sommer: *How do you think he should be remembered by the people of the state?*

Zdon: *As time goes by, I think, more and more affectionately. I think the bitterness that enveloped everything the last year or so that he was around will be forgiven and be forgotten.... I think his accomplishments were so amazing, that they will stand out for that. He really did a good job, I think, is what people will eventually remember. I think they will just remember his spirit. People were very affectionate towards him right up until the last two or three years, I would say. And I think that affection will come back. Especially in dying young. Relatively young. That will help his thing, too.*

I think when a historian looks back from the year 2080 or so and tries to look at Minnesota governors, he will have to be among the one or two best governors in the history of the state for a number of reasons. There are any number of ways. The way he brought women into the process. The way he built things and brought people and Super Bowls and education. He stressed education so much. And, "Jobs, Jobs, Jobs." They were political catch phrases, but they were also at the heart of what he tried to do and people will remember him for that." [11]

It's also useful as you wind up to ask interviewees if you have missed anything or overlooked some aspect of the topic or if they have any other thoughts to add. This gives them an opportunity to make final comments or add information that wasn't covered or that they may have forgotten earlier. Once again, you'll just have to use your own judgment if the interviewee raises a pertinent but otherwise ignored issue. Perhaps it's a topic that can be addressed fairly quickly. But if not, you might want to schedule a second interview. It's also important to communicate new, unanticipated information to project coordinators because it may reflect an aspect of the topic that other interviewers should know and ask questions about, too.

Don't Turn Off the Recorder Quite Yet

Before you go into "after the interview" mode, take a quick look back through your interview outline plus any notes you jotted down during the course of the interview. Make sure you covered all the material you wanted to ask about. This is also the time to verify jargon and acronyms and to check the spelling of names. Don't be surprised, however, if your interviewee isn't sure whether Aunt Ann's name was spelled *Ann* or *Anne*. Sometimes you can verify such information from other sources, and sometimes you can't. Do the best you can. Likewise with acronyms. Military acronyms in particular can be tricky, and sometimes acronyms from decades ago can be very difficult to verify. Often, interviewees themselves won't even know what the acronym means. Again, do the best you can. Whoever transcribes the interview will thank you.

When you finally turn off your recorder, you will feel a sense of exhilaration that your interview went well. Or perhaps you'll be a bit disappointed that your interviewee didn't seem to be thoroughly engaged with the process, didn't recall many interesting details, and couldn't tell very interesting stories. Or maybe you're annoyed with yourself for not phrasing questions as well as you could have and missing opportunities to ask follow-ups. Don't be dismayed. Your interviewing skills will improve the more interviews you do. And sometimes interviewees everyone thought would be terrific just aren't as articulate as you imagined they'd be, no matter how well you asked the questions. In all likelihood, if you went into the interview thoroughly prepared, you will have emerged with interesting new information that documents your community's history, making an important contribution for today and for years to come.

Have Fun

"The oral history interview is an amazing tool to record someone's warm and personal recollections, and a valuable way in which to record the past. Interviewers meet many interesting people, encounter poignant and amusing stories, and almost without exception are glad to have met the person interviewed. Keep a sense of humor and have fun!"

Catherine H. Ogden, Chairman, Greenwich Library Oral History Project [12]

CHAPTER 6

After the Interview

You've turned off your recording device and now you're finished. Right?

Sorry. You still have some critical tasks to complete before your oral history interview is truly done. Your next job is to make sure the important and interesting information you've just recorded remains accessible for future generations, in addition to being usable for whatever short-term purpose your project has in mind. Future accessibility is, after all, one of the important elements that separate oral history from other forms of recording stories.

Most of your tasks now will be determined by whatever decisions project planners made at the outset of the project in conjunction with the repository that will be accessioning your oral history materials. **Volume 5,** *After the Interview in Community Oral History*, provides detailed information related to these processing tasks. You'll want to follow the specific procedures that have been determined for your project. But this chapter will get you started on the process of turning an oral history interview into a document others can use.

Handle Immediate Post-Interview Tasks

As soon as the recorder is turned off, three things should happen. First, thank the interviewee. You'll want to follow up your verbal thanks with a written thank-you note later, but a sincere expression of appreciation for the important contribution your interviewee has made to the project is always in order. No need to gush or exaggerate. Even if the information turns out to be less useful than you originally expected—perhaps he just couldn't remember things or she just wasn't as articulate as you'd hoped—your narrator has at least given the gift of time, which is always important to acknowledge.

Second, complete the Legal Release Agreement. This is a critical step because, without the interviewee's permission, no public use can be made of the interview contents. The purpose of this form should already have been explained to the interviewee and reviewed at the outset of the interview, but be prepared to go over it again as needed. And remember, the interviewer also signs a Legal Release Agreement, using either this same form or a different one. Remember also that a Legal Release Agreement must be signed after each interview session; if you return for a follow-up interview, a second Legal Release Agreement will be used.

Third, answer any questions your interviewee might have about what happens next in the process. Remember not to make any promises you can't keep. For example, is a commemorative video planned? An exhibit at the local library? A presentation at the schools? Even if you're sure your interview will be the gem of the collection, it's never a good idea to tell people that their priceless words will take center stage—or will even be used—in the public presentation. You probably can't guarantee anything at this point, so don't risk disappointing your interviewee. Besides, whatever pride may be associated with such public recognition in the short term may, in fact, be outweighed by the long-term value of the interviewee's insights and information for generations yet to come.

Many projects include a simple camera in the interviewer's project kit so you can take a photo of the interviewee in the interview setting, even if the interview has been video recorded. Before you finish packing up your gear, take a basic head-shot photo of the interviewee, which can then be included with the interview files that ultimately are turned over to your repository.

You may encounter other important recordkeeping that needs to take place before you leave the interview. If the interviewee has offered to loan photos, scrapbooks, or other materials for copying as part of the interview master file, be sure to log each item on a Photograph and Memorabilia Receipt form, including complete identifying information, which the interviewee should be able to provide (see Figure 6.1). If the materials are to be copied and returned, let the interviewee know when he can expect to get them back. See the appendix in **Volume 1, *Introduction to Community Oral History*** for this form or go online to www.LCoastPress.com.

PHOTOGRAPH AND MEMORABILIA RECEIPT

PROJECT NAME

Jazz Atlanta Oral History Project

OWNER

Name

Joseph A. Browne

Address	**Phone/Email**
123 Elm Street	404-555-1111 (home)
Atlanta, Georgia 40401	404-555-2222 x. 1 (work)
	jb@aol.com

ITEM

Type	**Quantity**
Complete set of Atlanta Jazz Festival posters dating from the first year of the festival (1959)	53 posters

Detailed Description (Describe item and circumstances of loan)

Each year the Atlanta Jazz Festival commissions a local artist to create a Festival poster. Poster art work is used on festival materials for that year. This is a complete set of posters dating from the beginning of the Festival. The posters may be scanned for the Atlanta Public Library special collections; they must be returned to Joseph A. Browne no later than two months after this form is signed.

Associated Dates

1959-2012

Physical Condition

The posters are in full color with some fading on the older posters. All are in excellent condition. Years 1961, 1965, and 1978 have slight tears in the corners where tacks were put through them to hang them on an office wall.

Instructions for use

Credit the Atlanta Jazz Festival and the Atlanta Public Library when using the poster collection; high resolution scans are available from the festival office for publications purposes.

(continued on following page)

Figure 6.1. Sample—Photograph and Memorabilia Receipt

Figure 6.1. Sample—Photograph and Memorabilia Receipt *(continued)*

RETURNED	
Items returned by *(name)*: Lane Smith	
OWNER	**INTERVIEWER**
Name (print) Joseph A. Browne	**Name (print)** Lane Smith
Signature *(sign here)*	**Signature** *(sign here)*
Date *(enter date)*	**Date** *(enter date)*

Once the recordkeeping has been handled, it's time to pack up your gear. Keeping equipment and supplies in order will help others who share the equipment, and it will help you the next time you head out for an interview, saving time and frustration in the long run. Don't forget that extra extension cord you ran behind the interviewee's sofa. And remember to turn the interviewee's telephone back on if you silenced it before the interview. Just as you set up everything in a smooth, professional manner, it's a good practice to do the same now. Nothing says "incompetent" more than an interviewer who takes a scatterbrained approach to gathering up gear.

The Interviewee Keeps Talking

What do I do if my interviewee keeps talking and launches into another great story, even after I've started packing up my gear? Sometimes interviewees are so enthusiastic about the oral history interview that your mere presence has reminded them of many anecdotes they want to share. That's a nice kind of problem to have. You'll just have to use your good judgment. If the interviewee launches into another anecdote that's relevant to the focus of your project, you have two choices.

- Ask him to stop a moment while you set up your equipment again so you can record the additional information.
- Find out if there's another time you could come back for an additional interview session.

Whichever choice you make will depend on time commitments—your own, the interviewee's, and the project's. If, on the other hand, the new stories seem far afield from the focus of your oral history project, you might want to try graciously explaining that the project is limited to whatever theme you've been discussing and apologize for not being able to record everything the interviewee has to say. In most cases, such circumstances can be avoided if the nature of the project has been thoroughly explained in the first place. Under no circumstances should you indicate that you'll come back later to talk about the new topics unless you really plan to do so.

Keep in mind, that despite your best efforts to thoroughly research the topic before you go out for an interview, it is always possible that an interviewee may have unexpected information that sheds entirely different light on the issue. It's important to record that information, even if it means setting up your gear again or making arrangements for another interview session.

As soon as you return to headquarters—whether that is your home or the work space the project is using—make copies of the recorded interview. Project planners will have determined a protocol for this based on the oral history guideline of making multiple copies in multiple formats and keeping them in multiple places (that is, based on the LOCKSS principle—lots of copies keeps stuff safe). Generally, this would include copying the recording to a computer hard drive and making another copy on an external hard drive. The point is that you need to start right way making redundant copies of the recording to guard against possible technical failures that could mean the loss of the interview altogether. Oral historians, in other words, tend to think like an elderly gentleman you might know who wears both a belt and suspenders. See **Volume 5,** *After the Interview in Community Oral History*, for information on various approaches to making multiple copies of interviews. Make the copies and label them before doing any other processing. The original should be designated as the Master Recording and set aside for safekeeping.

Next, before any more time elapses, complete the Interview Summary form, including an outline of the interview content (see Figure 6.2 on the following page). You will already have gathered the biographical data you need to document the basic facts about the interviewee. But there also should be space on the form for you jot down a brief summary of material covered during the interview, which becomes an important tool for those who will be processing or cataloging the interviews for the repository.

INTERVIEW SUMMARY	
PROJECT NAME Jazz Atlanta Oral History Project	**INTERVIEW ID#** *(insert interview ID number)*
INTERVIEWEE	**INTERVIEWER**
NAME (as it will appear in the public record) Joseph A. Browne 123 Elm Street Atlanta, Georgia 30301	**NAME** Lane Smith 890 Oak Street Atlanta, Georgia 30305
CONTACT 404-555-1111 (home) 404-555-2222 x. 1 (work) jb@aol.com	**CONTACT** 404-666-1111 ls@aol.com
OTHER NAMES KNOWN BY Joey Browne	
INTERVIEW DATE *(insert)*	**INTERVIEW LENGTH** 90 minutes
RECORDING MEDIUM <u>X</u> digital audio _digital video	
DELIVERY MEDIUM <u>X</u> sound file <u>X</u> sound card _ CD _DVD	
TECHNICAL NOTES (make/model of recorder, format recorded, microphone notes) The interview was recorded on a Marantz PMD 620 with SD Flash Media using lavaliere microphones.	
INTERVIEW NOTES (physical environment, interviewee's mood, people or animals in the room, interruptions) The interview was recorded in the Atlanta Jazz Festival director's office. Mr. Browne was interested in doing the interview and was prepared for it. He had a number of questions before the interview began and said the topical outline sent to him prior to the interview was very helpful in organizing his thoughts. He was comfortable with the questions asked and added information pertinent to the project at the end of the interview.	

(Continued on following page)

Figure 6.2. Sample—Interviewee Summary Form

Figure 6.2. Sample—Interviewee Summary Form *(continued)*

DATE LEGAL RELEASE AGREEMENT SIGNED
(date signed/should match the interview date)

PROPER NAMES AND KEYWORDS
(personal and place names with proper spelling, dates, and keywords)

See the attached list of proper and place names the interviewer jotted down during the interview. Mr. Browne checked the spelling of the names at the end of the interview.

SUMMARY OF INTERVIEW CONTENT

During the interview, Mr. Browne discussed:
- His background, education, and early interest in jazz
- His choice of instrument and his musical education
- His description of southern musical traditions
- His musical influences, the roots of some of these influences in musical traditions in the American South, and his thoughts about the influences
- His decision to take a position with the Atlanta Jazz Festival
- The role of the Atlanta Jazz Festival in Atlanta, in Georgia, and in the American South
- Stories of jazz greats who have participated in the festival
- Thoughts about the future of the festival
- Thoughts about the future of jazz traditions in the American South

COMPLETED BY	DATE
Lane Smith	*(insert date)*

Additionally, the Interview Summary form allows you to document the context of the interview, another characteristic of oral histories that sets them apart from other kinds of recorded information. Make sure the Interview Summary includes sufficient detail on why this person was interviewed and the importance of what the person said. It's never appropriate to be an armchair psychologist, but untoward events like job losses, death in the family, or serious illnesses can affect an interviewee's perspective and, if known, should be noted as a fact that future users of the interview might want to take into account.

Interview Summary Example

Here's what an interview summary prepared immediately after the interview might look like.

Interview with the Rev. Joe Barnes, Lutheran parsonage on County Road 97A, July 11, 2012

- Barnes described upbringing in the county; discussed leaving for seminary at age 18

- Decided to return home after ordination in 2002 because many area residents were unchurched and he felt he was needed here

- Reconnected with Doris Fleming, childhood sweetheart; they married and now have two children, Abraham, 4, and Zachariah, 2

- Describes congregation's goals of reaching out to families in county who don't seem to belong anywhere

- Recounts notable successes with people in northwest section of county

- Expresses frustration with how long it takes to gain people's trust

- Says congregation has built community by being there for each other after tornado two years ago severely damaged properties in NE part of county; notes it was God's blessing no one was killed or even severely injured

- Describes work teams that helped with clean-up, even if people weren't members of congregation

- Says congregation has grown from 53 families to 97 families since he's been here, despite the population not increasing that much (check details on pop.; add footnote to transcript)

- Reflects on how some people he was in seminary with seem to find it amusing that he's challenged by staying in a rural church but says he wouldn't have it any other way

You can establish context for the interview by thinking about the following questions and noting any relevant details on the Interview Summary form.

CREATE CONTEXT FOR THE INTERVIEW

✓ How does the interview fit into the project's overall documentation effort?

✓ Did notable surprises emerge?

✓ What about any extenuating circumstances that might affect the person's answers or even the nature of the interview itself?

✓ Did you form any impressions about the nature of the exchange? Did the person seem reluctant? Eager? Emotional? Disengaged? Enthusiastic about sharing?

From time to time, something an interviewer finds particularly noteworthy occurs during an interview that requires a more detailed contextual discussion. Write it down now, before you forget. It's almost impossible to provide too much information for the record.

Documenting Circumstances of an Interview

Here's what an interviewer's additional notes documenting the context of the interview might look like.

When I arrived at the Farm Crisis Hotline offices, the interviewee, Mrs. Clouse, said the volunteer who was supposed to man the hotline today called in and said a family emergency would prevent her from coming in. So Mrs. Clouse explained she'd have to listen for the phone, but she didn't expect to get too many calls today. The first time a call came in, I paused the recorder and then started it again when she finished the conversation. I did that the second and third time too. But after that, I kept it running and recorded her side of the phone calls. She never addressed someone by their full name, and often didn't even say that, so I figured we weren't invading anyone's privacy. Also I observed during the first couple of (unrecorded) calls that you could learn a lot about Mrs. Clouse from the way she dealt with people sympathetically and by the kinds of available services and places to get help that she described to callers. While she was talking to the callers, I got ideas for other questions to ask that we hadn't anticipated during the preparation phase, so I was able to build on those calls to enrich the interview. It's also interesting to hear how her voice reflects her concerns about these people, but she seems determined not to become discouraged, despite the limitations on what the crisis center can actually do to alleviate farmers' financial problems.

A number of post-interview tasks remain before the interview can be turned over to the repository. Projects might choose to handle these in various ways, as outlined in **Volume 5,** *After the Interview in Community Oral History*, but interviewers might be expected to do some, or all, of the tasks described in the following sections.

Transcribe the Interview

Sometimes volunteers or paid transcribers will perform this task; other times, the interviewers will do it. Computer software for transcribing allows you to easily start and stop the play-back of an audio interview so you can type word for word what the interviewee and the interviewer said. Interviews that are video recorded also should be transcribed in the same way so the audio component can be preserved as a text document.

Project teams or directors will decide the format and style for transcribing, so all the interviews in the project collection will have a consistent appearance. The project teams also will develop a transcribing standard for dealing with circumstances like inaudible words and phrases. Some projects, for example, tell transcribers to listen to such a passage three times and then move on, leaving blanks in the transcript. This is less of a problem if interviewers are transcribing their own interviews, because they can usually recall what the interviewee said, even if it isn't abundantly clear on the recording.

It's worth noting that sometimes, even if the sound quality on the recording is good, an interviewee may have a rapid or indistinct speaking style that makes understanding parts of the interview challenging for someone who wasn't there. While you may plan to rely on the recording for research purposes, it can still be helpful to prepare a transcript while the interview is fresh. Otherwise, future listeners may be hard-pressed to understand everything on the recording, which increases the possibility of misquoting or misinterpreting what your interviewee said.

Project directors also will decide how the interview should be indexed for future reference, a process that may be the responsibility of the transcriber or may be a task handled later by others. The transcription process is covered in detail in **Volume 5,** *After the Interview in Community Oral History.*

If the interviewers in your project will not be expected to transcribe the interviews, they still should be expected to help those performing this task by providing correct spellings of proper names and other unfamiliar terms the interviewee uses. Use your interview notes to create an alphabetical list of these names and words to turn over with the recording. It can save countless hours in the long run if the person transcribing the interview gets the spellings right the first time rather than having to make corrections later.

Audit Check the Transcript

No matter who transcribes the interview, the interviewer always should audit check the transcript. This involves carefully listening to the recorded interview while following along on the transcript, making corrections as you go along. Even the most carefully prepared transcript may contain errors that can be caught on the audit check. Keep in mind that the goal throughout this process is accuracy, and a faithful transcript is critical to achieving that goal.

Arrange for Copying and Transfer of Artifacts and Legal Release Agreements

Creating the paper trail that documents each interview and any accompanying artifacts begins with the interviewer. Make sure Legal Release Agreements are properly filled out and signed before turning them over to the person designated to handle the paperwork. Likewise, if the interviewee has loaned scrapbooks or photos to be copied, make sure that process is handled promptly so the materials can be returned in a timely manner. If the interviewee wants to donate objects, make sure the appropriate documentation accompanies each item, so the museum or other repository taking the donations has an authentic paper trail for its records.

Prepare Your Notes About the Interview Content and Context

Review the notes you made right after your interview and add any additional information that would be helpful for future users of the interview. Did some new insight occur to you when you were audit checking the transcript? Do you have suggestions if anyone does follow-up interviews in the future?

Collect All Your Interview Materials for the Repository

Working with the repository where your interviews will be deposited, your project director will have a checklist of all the items that the repository will expect to accompany a fully processed interview. Again, see **Volumes 2, Volume 3,** and **Volume 5** of the *Toolkit* for detailed information.

ITEMS TO ACCOMPANY AN INTERVIEW

✓ correspondence with the interviewee

✓ research notes

✓ your question outline and notes jotted during the interview

✓ the signed Legal Release Agreement

✓ a photo of the interviewee

✓ the transcript

✓ the Interview Summary form, which will be used in cataloging, preservation, and publicity about the project

OK. Now you're finished. You've created an archival quality oral history interview that documents a specific aspect of the history of your community.

The project team may have considerable work left to do if creating public programming is part of your project's goal. Portions of the interviews may be destined for Web publication. Or perhaps they will become grist for a theatrical performance or traveling museum exhibit. Maybe you'll see them published in a book or turned into newspaper articles. Possibly local teachers will incorporate them into their history lessons. Whatever the immediate use may be, rest assured you and your interviewee have created an important piece of documentation about your community in a particular time and place, something that future scholars and community members would not have otherwise. And that may be the most important contribution of all.

NOTES

1. El Toro Marine Corps Air Station Oral History Project. Response to *Community Oral History Toolkit* questionnaire. March 2009.

2. Rocky Flats Oral History Project, Maria Rogers Oral History Program, Carnegie Branch Library for Local History of the Boulder (CO) Public Library. Response to *Community Oral History Toolkit* questionnaire. March 2009.

3. *Tod's Point, Greenwich, Connecticut: An Oral History, 2nd ed.* (Greenwich, CT: The Greenwich Library, 2000): 29, 31.

4. May O. White interview transcript. Worcester Women's History Project. http://www.wwhp.org/activities-exhibits/oral-history-project/interview-list/may-white. Accessed May 31, 2012.

5. Mary Kay Quinlan and Barbara W. Sommer, *The People Who Made It Work: A Centennial Oral History of the Cushman Motor Works.* (Lincoln, NE: Textron, Inc., 2001): 1-2.

6. James A. Ballentine. *Ballentine's Law Dictionary, 3rd ed.* (Rochester, NY: The Lawyer's Co-Operative Publishing Co., 1969): 272.

7. *Tod's Point, Greenwich, Connecticut: An Oral History, 2nd ed.* (Greenwich, CT: The Greenwich Library, 2000): 8.

8. Information about the Obama Volunteers Story Project in Arapahoe County, CO, is taken from a presentation at the Oral History Association conference in Atlanta, Oct. 29, 2010. Cyns Nelson provided a copy of the interview outline the project used.

9. "Liberty School," www.blandcountyhistoryarchives.org/libertyoneroom. html#anchor130873. Accessed May 31, 2012.

10. Alan T. Zdon Oral History Transcript. Governor Rudy Perpich Oral History Project. Iron Range Research Center Archival Collections. http://ironrange. cdmhost.com/cdm/ref/collection/p202901coll2/id/42. Accessed May 31, 2012.

11. Ibid.

12. Greenwich Library Oral History Project. Response to *Community Oral History Toolkit* questionnaire. March 2009.

Volume 1 of the *Community Oral History Toolkit* contains a comprehensive list of resources to guide oral history practitioners through all steps of the oral history process. The following list includes a variety of guides to oral history theory and practice for those interested in further exploration of topics raised in this volume. Also included are examples of some of the many hundreds of publications, including websites, that use oral history interviews. The resources listed here are primarily examples cited in this volume, but online interviews abound, from projects created by elementary and secondary students to those published by major academic institutions. Taking a look at interviews from other projects may offer ideas not only about how to conduct oral history interviews—and how not to conduct them—but also about how to share them for public use.

Guides to Oral History Theory and Practice

Baylor Institute for Oral History http://www.baylor.edu/oralhistory/index.php?id=23560

MacKay, Nancy. *Curating Oral Histories: From Interview to Archive.* Walnut Creek, CA: Left Coast Press, Inc., 2007.

Mercier, Laurie and Madeline Buckendorf. *Using Oral History in Community History Projects.* Carlisle, PA: Oral History Association, 2007.

Nebraska State Historical Society, "Capturing the Living Past: An Oral History Primer" http://nebraskahistory.org/lib-arch/research/audiovis/oral_history/

Neuenschwander, John A. *A Guide to Oral History and the Law.* New York, Oxford University Press, 2009.

Ritchie, Donald A. *Doing Oral History: A Practical Guide,* 2nd ed. New York: Oxford University Press, 2003.

Ritchie, Donald A., Ed. *The Oxford Handbook of Oral History.* New York: Oxford University Press, 2011.

Sommer, Barbara W. and Mary Kay Quinlan. *The Oral History Manual,* 2nd ed. Lanham, MD: AltaMira Press, 2009.

Trimble, Charles E., Barbara W. Sommer, and Mary Kay Quinlan. *The American*

Indian Oral History Manual: Making Many Voices Heard. Walnut Creek, CA: Left Coast Press, Inc., 2008.

Yow, Valerie Raleigh. *Recording Oral History: A Guide for the Humanities and Social Sciences,* 2nd ed. Walnut Creek, CA: AltaMira Press, 2005.

Using Oral History Interviews

Columbia University Oral History Research Office, *Stories from the Collection,* DVD. New York: Columbia University, 1998.

Making Sense of Oral History. History Matters: The U.S. Survey Course on the Web. http://historymatters.gmu.edu/mse/oral

Minnesota Historical Society, Minnesota's Greatest Generation Website http://stories.mnhs.org/mgg/index.html

Portelli, Alessandro. *The Order Has Been Carried Out: History, Memory, and Meaning of a Nazi Massacre in Rome.* New York, Palgrave Macmillan, 2007.

Rocky Gap (VA) High School, http://www.blandcountyhistoryarchives.org

Sommer, Barbara W. *Hard Work and a Good Deal: The Civilian Conservation Corps in Minnesota.* Minnesota Historical Society Press, 2008.

Special Collections, Carnegie Branch Library for Local History of the Boulder (CO) Public Library http://www.boulderlibrary.org/oralhistory/

Tod's Point, Greenwich, Connecticut: An Oral History, 2nd ed. Greenwich, CT: The Greenwich Library, 2000.

INDEX

ABOUT THE AUTHORS

Mary Kay Quinlan, Ph.D., is an associate professor at the University of Nebraska-Lincoln in the College of Journalism and Mass Communications. She has held positions at the University of Maryland, and has served as president of the National Press Club. She is editor of the Oral History Association Newsletter and co-author with Barbara Sommer of *The Oral History Manual*, 2nd ed. (AltaMira Press, 2009), *Native American Veterans Oral History Manual* (Nebraska Foundation for the Preservation of Oral History, 2005), and *Discovering Your Connections to History* (AASLH, 2000). She is also a co-author with Sommer and Charles E. Trimble of *The American Indian Oral History Manual: Making Many Voices Heard* (Left Coast Press, Inc., 2008).

Nancy MacKay, MLIS, has been straddling the line between libraries and oral history for more than twenty years. As a librarian she has worked with special collections, cataloging, and music in various academic settings. As an oral historian she teaches, consults, advises, and writes about oral history, especially oral history and archives. She directed the oral history program at Mills College, from 2001-2011, and currently teaches library science and oral history at San Jose State University. Nancy is the author of *Curating Oral Histories* (Left Coast Press, Inc., 2007).

Barbara W. Sommer, M.A., has more than thirty-five years' experience in the oral history field. She has been principal investigator and director of more than twenty major oral history projects and has taught at the University of Nebraska-Lincoln, Nebraska Wesleyan University, and Vermilion Community College, MN. She is author of many key publications in the field, including, with Mary Kay Quinlan, *The Oral History Manual*, 2nd ed. (AltaMira Press, 2009) and with Quinlan and Charles E. Trimble, *The American Indian Oral History Manual: Making Many Voices Heard* (Left Coast Press, Inc., 2008). Her award-winning book *Hard Work and a Good Deal: The Civilian Conservation Corps in Minnesota* (Minnesota Historical Society Press, 2008) draws on oral history interviews about the Civilian Conservation Corps.